RUNNING
for Health and Beauty

RUNNING
for Health and Beauty

A Complete Guide for Women

by Kathryn Lance

THE BOBBS-MERRILL COMPANY, INC.
Indianapolis   New York

Designed by Ingrid Beckman
Manufactured in the United States of America

Eighth Printing

Library of Congress Cataloging in Publication Data

Lance, Kathryn.
    Running for health and beauty.

    Includes index.
    1. Exercise for women.   2. Running.   3. Women—
Health and hygiene.   I. Title.
RA781.L29   613.7′1   76-45576
ISBN 0-672-52252-7

To Robert Cenedella, who, like Charlotte, is a true friend and a good writer

Acknowledgments

THIS book would not have been possible without the generous help of my two consultants, Edward Colt, M.D., and Bob Glover, Physical Director of the West Side YMCA. Both men, who are runners as well as experts on running, provided me with much valuable information and advice, and both read the manuscript for medical and physiological accuracy. I want to thank them for the time they took from their own busy schedules of work and running to help prepare a book that we hope will benefit all beginning women runners.

I would also like to thank Dr. Richard Schuster and Dr. Ernst van Aaken, whose excellent informal talks at the West Side YMCA provided me with much valuable material; and certainly Joe Henderson, Dr. George Sheehan, and the other editors and writers of *Runner's World* magazine, which is by far the best source of information on all aspects of running.

Many other people helped in the preparation of this book; like all authors, I wish I had space to thank them all by name. Those who were particularly helpful include Joe Kleinerman, of the New York City Road Runners Club, who helped me find race results and other esoteric bits of information; Lee Kantor, of the West Side YMCA, for his advice and encouragement; Arno Niemand, whose enthusiasm and sponsorship have made the Mini-Marathon an annual event; and Dee Howell, Physical Director of the Rome, New York, YMCA, who gave me a great deal of information and introduced me to some of the women runners in her program. I would also like to thank the dozens of women runners who answered my questionnaires and submitted to interviews, particularly Trina Hosmer, Paula Davenport, Ruth Baker, Virginia Murling, and above all Nina Kuscsik, who is one of the pioneers of modern women's running.

Very special thanks go to my good friend and running partner, Fern Budow, who was my first convert, and to Bill Taxerman, who introduced me to running. And of course thanks to all my friends, runners and nonrunners, who have encouraged me throughout the preparation of this book, and listened when I talked about nothing but running for weeks on end. I would especially like to mention Maury Kurtz, Jim Forsht, Nan Schubel, Terry Wolf, Ted Cmarada, Mary K. Erie, Dave McKay, Simon Barsky, John Sposato, Gene Busnar, and my parents, John F. and Kathryn H. Lance.

Finally, I want to thank Diane Giddis, my excellent and conscientious editor, for her good judgment and the many hours of hard work she has devoted to this book.

Contents

Introduction

SUPPOSE there were a treatment you could take that would do the following things:

—help you lose weight and keep it off
—streamline your figure
—improve your complexion
—help you give up smoking
—help you sleep better
—make you less nervous
—increase your energy
—improve your digestion
—keep your hands and feet warm, even in winter

Would you take such a treatment? Sure you would—no matter what it cost or where you had to go for it. Well, believe it or not, there is such a treatment, and it is readily available and practically free. That "treatment" is a simple physical exercise: running. If you follow the programs in this book, within weeks you may begin to notice all the benefits listed above—and more. And you will achieve them with a minimum expenditure of effort, money, and time.

Your only investment in money will be the cost of a pair of good running shoes, and perhaps a pair of shorts. Your investment in effort is up to you; but, speaking from experience, I can assure you that the effort expended to run regularly is far less than that required to stick to any kind of calisthenics program. And the investment in time? As little as four hours a week.

Skeptical? I don't blame you. But read on. No matter how fat, lazy, out of condition or generally hopeless you think you are, I was in worse shape when I started running four years ago. So keep reading and see how running changed my life—and learn how it could change yours.

1

How Running Transformed My Life

IN 1972, at the age of twenty-nine, I had a high-pressure desk job that meant hours of sitting on my spreading fanny, at least two packs of cigarettes a day and constant munching. Not surprisingly, I was irritable and depressed, and troubled by insomnia. My color was bad, my skin a mass of discolored spots. I couldn't climb a flight of stairs without wheezing. In short, I was a physical wreck.

From time to time I would embark on an exercise program, which usually amounted to about three days of trying to do the Canadian Air Force exercises. Once I even enrolled in a "stretchercise" class for working women. I stuck with this for about six months, at the end of which time I could bend over and touch my toes without undue pain, but my general fitness level still left a great deal to be desired.

Actually, I had never been what you would call really fit. In grade school I was always the last person chosen for a team. In high school

I avoided gym by claiming that it was my period about two weeks out of every month. And in college my gym classes consisted of such courses as billiards and folk dancing. After all, physical activity wasn't ladylike—it only made you grunt and sweat.

By my late twenties, when some of my friends began to complain about suddenly flabby thighs or a bulging tummy, I only smiled. I had never known a time in my life when my thighs weren't flabby and my stomach didn't sag. At last everyone else was catching up with me. So what if my muscle tone resembled overcooked linguini? That was the natural order of things. So, too, I reasoned, were the crow's-feet at the outer corners of my eyes and the worry lines in my forehead. After all, I could always save my money and have a face lift in another few years.

As for my rotten disposition—well, that's just the way I was. I kept promising myself I would improve my health habits and maybe even give up smoking someday—but there was no rush. After all, I was still young—only in my late twenties. Right?

Wrong. My calendar age was twenty-nine, which, while not exactly that of a child, was hardly old. But my body was aging far faster than I realized. Just how fast became clear when increasingly frequent headaches and general blahs finally drove me to a doctor for a physical checkup.

"You're not in very good condition," the doctor told me, puffing on his own cigarette. "But there's nothing really wrong with you. Your blood pressure is a little elevated—175 over 90."

I stared at him. Nothing really wrong? A *little* elevated? I knew that normal blood pressure for a woman my age was more like 130 over 80. What should I do?

"Stop worrying," said the doctor. "Cut down on your salt. Exercise. Stop smoking. And come back in a few months. If you're still elevated, we can put you on medication."

To say I was shook is putting it mildly. I had thought of high blood pressure as an old person's disease. (It's not, really—statistics show that it is increasing dramatically among teen-agers and persons in their twenties. Doctors believe this may be due in part to sedentary life styles and diets high in salt and refined sugar.) I knew that high blood pressure can lead to stroke. I also knew that many of its sufferers must stay on medication all their lives. I had visions of spending the rest of my life as a semi-invalid.

But what to do about it? Well, the doctor had said to exercise. But I'd already tried that, and I knew I couldn't stick to a program. Besides, it seemed unlikely that touching my toes would appreciably help my circulatory system. I finally remembered that a friend had told me his blood pressure went down when he started jogging. Maybe I should look into that.

I went to my neighborhood bookstore to look for books on running. I was astonished to find very few. Most of them seemed to have been written for people who had once been active in sports and wanted to stay in condition, or they were technical manuals for those interested in professional or Olympic track events. None of the books were written for women. Nevertheless, I bought the books available, modified their principles as well as I could, and started slowly.

At first I tried running in place indoors. After only two days, the man downstairs threatened to call the police. Besides, it was boring, and it hurt my ankles, so I went outside and tried running around the block.

This was no good, either. For one thing, I couldn't run one full block without stepping in something; and for another, running in front of the street people, who were always hanging around and snickering, made me self-conscious.

Finally I joined the local YMCA. And that's when my life began to really change. The Y had an indoor track that ran around the top of the gymnasium, twenty-four laps to the mile. At the time I joined, there were only a handful of other women members; today there are hundreds.

And, yes, there were hassles. A lot of the gay men didn't want any women in "their" Y, and they made catty remarks to that effect. The straight men amused themselves by whistling and calling out such comments as: "What'cha running from, baby?" or "If I catch you, can I keep you?" Whenever I found myself getting annoyed, I just remembered my blood pressure and the amount of money I had paid to join the Y and I kept running.

When I started I could run only four laps without getting out of breath. That was quite discouraging, so I decided that if I didn't show any improvement after three weeks, I would stop. What did I have to lose? For the next three weeks I forced myself to go to the Y four times a week. Miraculously, at the end of that time, I found I could run six laps without tiring. A quarter of a mile! I had actually improved! And I was not only running farther but actually smoking less, and without any conscious effort.

Now seemed the time to cut out cigarettes altogether, and so I did—cold turkey. It wasn't easy. But it wasn't as painful as I had expected, either. The running really had made it easier, by improving my lung capacity and keeping me calm.

At the same time I stopped smoking, I changed my running program and started aiming for a full mile. I would run until tired, then walk, then run again until I had completed the twenty-four laps. For the next few weeks, I couldn't run more than six continuous laps without tiring. Then gradually I became able to run more and more laps. Finally, in late November, on my thirtieth birthday, I put it all together and ran one full mile without stopping!

By January I was up to two miles. And late in May of that same year I entered the Women's Mini-Marathon in Central Park, a full six-mile race, and finished in 56 minutes. From total slob to track star in approximately nine months!

So now I could run six miles without stopping. So what?

Well, for one thing, my blood pressure had dropped to 110 over 65.

My pulse rate, a measure of healthy heart and lungs, was also down—to about 65. But the other effects were what really made the difference. Some of these had been immediate; some I noticed only gradually (and I am *still* noticing new benefits, the longer I run).

Almost immediately, after I had been running only two weeks, I found I slept better and had more energy. A few months later, I noticed that I was actually sleeping about one hour *less* a night, but waking up more refreshed and ready to go.

Within six weeks I was no longer smoking and no longer wanted to smoke. My feet were no longer cold at night. I was never constipated. My skin was clearer, and the frown lines seemed to have disappeared. I could eat anything I wanted without gaining weight.

My disposition was far better. I no longer flew off the handle at little things (well, hardly ever). I was much less nervous. After a hard day of working at my desk, I would go to the Y, start running, and feel the tension melt away from my neck and shoulders. My posture was better, and my general appearance was so much improved that friends and co-workers were convinced I had a secret lover.

One year after I started running, my body had completely changed. Of course I had expected my legs to change—they quickly became much more shapely as my calves filled out and my thighs slimmed down. But I had also lost ten pounds without dieting at all. My dress size had shrunk from a 14 to a 10. Incredibly, my bust had gone from a 34A to a 36B. (Other women runners have noticed the same thing—apparently the action of the arms improves the tone of the pectoral muscles, which support the breasts.)

One night when I was taking a shower I realized that I wasn't flabby *anywhere*; legs, buttocks, tummy, upper arms—all were firm and smooth. For a moment I had the spooky feeling that I was dressed up in somebody else's body.

I wasn't the only one who noticed these changes. As a girlfriend was helping me pick out my first bikini one afternoon, she suddenly sighed. "I can't believe it," she said. "Your body looks fabulous."

At my annual checkup my gynecologist told me my muscle tone was better than that of most teen-age girls.

But I got the best compliment of all from an old boyfriend I hadn't seen since college. When I first heard he was coming to town I was somewhat nervous, wondering if we would still have anything in common. As it happened, I needn't have worried, because we took up almost where we had left off years before. The last thing he said before he left was, "If I hadn't seen it, I wouldn't have believed it. Your body is great. In fact, you're in better shape than you were when you were eighteen." And believe me—he knew.

Aside from effecting all the obvious physical changes, running improved my self-confidence tremendously. Part of it, I think, had to do with my increased calmness and energy. But part of it was also from finding out what I was capable of physically. I was a real "jockette" now—and loving every minute of it. My only regret was that I hadn't started running when I was much younger.

The same thing can be true for you. I guarantee that if you follow one of the programs in the next chapter—and really give it a fair try—you can change your own appearance, your body, your disposition, and your life.

2

Why Run?

Women and Sports

You have been cheated. Throughout your entire life, your family, your schools, society itself—all have systematically cheated you of one of your most fundamental rights: the right to a healthy, active body.

Studies show that girls tend to reach their peak of physical fitness at about age thirteen or fourteen—and from there on it's straight downhill. Is this because women are innately less athletic than men? No, it's because from the time we are very young, our culture simply doesn't encourage females to take care of their bodies. Worse, in subtle and not-so-subtle ways, we are actually discouraged from using our bodies in a truly athletic way.

Turn on the television set on any Sunday afternoon and chances are you'll see a sports program: baseball, football, basketball. The members of the teams are all men. The sports commentators are mostly men.

Take a walk around your neighborhood. Pass by a schoolyard any afternoon. What do you see? In one corner of the schoolyard, a softball game; in another, a basketball game. All of the players, or most of them, are boys. Sometimes you will see girls in these games, but seldom more than one or two. If your neighborhood schoolyard is anything like mine, the few teen-age girls in the yard are sitting nearby, talking together, watching the boys, perhaps smoking cigarettes. Occasionally a girl will attempt to hit a softball, usually accompanied by squeals from the other girls and derisive laughter from the boys. If she does manage to hit the ball, she usually giggles and goes back to the sidelines, because she can't run to first base in her high wedgie shoes.

Pick up the sports section of your daily newspaper. Besides reports of games and events—mostly played by men—there are after-game interviews in the locker room. What kind of image does that bring to mind? Happy, exhausted men, downing a beer, toweling off, in that forbidden, almost mystical camaraderie of men's sports. Most men know that this camaraderie is one of the basic pleasures of any sports activity—it's the end result of going off with your friends, having some fun, working up a sweat, and then relaxing together.

The image of women's sports is entirely different. With a few isolated exceptions, it is only very recently that women athletes have been popularly accepted at all, mostly through the efforts of Billie Jean King and other tennis stars. But even then, when you think about women tennis players, who first comes to mind? Perhaps Chris Evert, who is a great athlete, but whom the news media present as a cool, collected, dainty and feminine young woman in pastel tennis skirts who probably doesn't sweat at all. And can you imagine Chrissie, Billie, and Evonne sitting around in the locker room after a tennis match, swapping stories and downing a few? Of course not. The whole idea seems somehow distasteful and a little . . . well, unnatural.

Certainly the image of women's sports is beginning to change: besides tennis, women's gymnastics and track are beginning to attract a great deal of media attention. But young girls still have far fewer athletic roles to aspire to than little boys; even though a young girl might play on a baseball team, she would probably never dream of aiming for the major leagues, because she has internalized the idea that all female athletes are inferior to all male athletes. Though it's true that in sports requiring muscular strength the best woman will probably never be quite so good as the best man, women can and do compete with men on equal terms in many sports, from volleyball to tennis. Furthermore, in contests involving agility or endurance, chances are the best woman could outperform the best man: most of the world's long-distance swimming records, for instance, are held by women. But perhaps because ice skating, long-distance swimming, and other sports in which women excel have not been so highly publicized as such male-dominated sports as football and basketball, too many people in our society retain the old image: women don't run and kick balls, women don't compete aggressively, women don't sweat.

In fact, we don't even perspire if we can help it, thanks to commercials and advertisements which equate dampness with social disease. The truth is that there are two kinds of sweat: "nervous" sweat and "work" sweat, the kind that's caused by vigorous exercise. A good, healthy sweat is a sign that your body is working at its maximum capacity, doing what it was designed to do: being active.

You've probably heard all this before. You know you should get more exercise. You've probably also read articles which deplore modern household appliances. Such appliances, these articles say, are responsible for the poor physical condition of most American women. Before dishwashers and vacuum cleaners, women got plenty of exercise washing clothes by hand, taking care of a ten-room house, baking their own bread. The implication seems to be that women should go back to doing these things if they want to be healthy. Become more active, these articles urge us. Do stretching exercises while you sweep. Walk to the supermarket. Hang out your wet clothes on the line.

Apart from the fact that most women today work outside the home and don't have time for such meaningless drudgery, what these articles don't tell you is that exercise should fulfill two functions. The first is that it should be vigorous enough to make you breathe hard and break out in a sweat; the second, and just as important, is that exercise should make you feel good. You should enjoy it. Those pro ball players on TV are making a lot of money, but they also enjoy what they do. Your husband or lover may go to the Y twice a week to play handball or basketball to keep in shape, but he also does it because he enjoys it, because it is fun.

He does it because he knows something that you have probably never had a chance to find out, or that you have forgotten: strenuous physical activity makes you feel terrific. Sweating is great. Pushing yourself to your physical limits and then relaxing afterwards, taking a hot shower, feeling your body throb and tingle all over—this is one of the most pleasurable experiences of life. I know that may be a little hard to believe; four years ago I would probably have been skeptical too. But for sheer overall pleasure of mind, body and spirit, nothing beats the feeling of relaxing after a strenuous physical workout. I'd rank it as one of the top three sensual pleasures, right up there with great sex and great food.

Why don't you know this? Well, think back to the last time you were really active on a consistent basis. It was probably in grade school, or high school at the latest. What PE courses did you take? The only active course I ever took in high school was field hockey. I thought it was a lot of fun and would have liked to continue playing it—but it was offered for only six weeks, three weeks of which were spent learning the rules. Most of the rest of my formal physical education was spent sampling such "sports" as modern dance and rifle. Meanwhile, the boys in my school were playing vigorous team sports or were involved in track and field activities—and they were playing all year long, not just six weeks at a time.

If your experience was similar to mine, the most popular boys in your school were probably the star athletes—the ace pitcher, the cute quarterback, the quarter-miler. And the most popular girls? The cheerleaders and pom-pom girls. I'm not putting down the things these girls did. In my school some of these girls were athletes in their own right—one was a state-ranked swimmer, and the head pom-pom girl went on to become a professional ballerina. The routines they learned took agility, control, and strength. But most of the work these girls did was not vigorous sport, the kind that works up a good body sweat. Worse, leading cheers and doing pom-pom routines are not the kinds of sports you can continue your whole life. The former center of my high school's basketball team still goes to the gym to work out with his buddies a few times a week. But can you imagine the head cheerleader, a thirty-five-year-old accountant, going out in the park to run through a few cheers with her friends? Once a physically active person, she was deprived of the chance to learn a sport she could play for her whole life. If she has continued to be active, it is almost certainly through her own efforts—because in our society women are not expected to continue sports into their adult lives, no matter how active they were as children.

Today almost everyone agrees that women have a right to earn as much money as men for equal work. But where you stand on the question of woman's place in society is irrelevant. For whether you are a superior being, man's equal, or a creature formed from Adam's rib to serve him, the most basic fact about you is that your body was made for lifelong physical activity—and that is why I say you have been cheated. If, like most women, you stopped regular physical activity long ago, you've been missing out on one of the most important, basic, and rewarding parts of your life.

Institutionalized discrimination against women's sports is beginning to change. In 1975, HEW ruled that public school districts would no longer be eligible for federal funds unless they provided girls the same opportunities for physical education as they provide boys. As more girls learn more sports, more will demand the opportunity to play these sports as adults.

Maybe by the time our daughters are grown, then, it will be routine for women to participate in physical activity throughout their lives. But that schoolyard in my neighborhood is still almost one hundred percent male. In fact, only once have I seen a little girl even attempt to play basketball. She was about six years old, and the big boys kept knocking her ball away from her and laughing at her. With the quiet dignity that only a six-year-old can muster, she doggedly retrieved her ball each time and went back to the hoop. She never did manage actually to sink a basket, but maybe she'll make it yet.

I don't mean to imply here that American men as a whole are in good physical condition. You have only to look around you to see that they aren't. In fact, the beer belly, the premature paunch, and flabby, overweight arms and legs are the norm for most Americans of both sexes. For most of my life I simply didn't tune in to this reality. But once I had become a runner, I became more aware of the physical condition of those around me. As far as I'm concerned, nothing is a bigger turnoff now than a man who is out of condition, no matter how charming, witty, or intelligent he is. In general, though, most men are in much better shape than most women, because men engage in more activity for a longer period of their lives.

The older a woman is, in fact, the harder it is for her to start and to stick with an exercise program. Moreover, Dr. Joan Ullyot, a marathon runner and nationally known exercise physician, says even young women have as much difficulty as men in their forties in starting an exercise program. Since most women stop being physically active at the age of ten or twelve, muscular atrophy starts to set in at about twenty instead of forty, as with most men. But—and this is the good news—no matter how old or out of shape you are, running can get you back into good shape—the shape you were meant to be in.

Or suppose you're one of the few women in our society who have remained active in sports as adults. Perhaps you're on a company softball team, or you play tennis every weekend. Running is still a good exercise for you, one that will improve your game noticeably. Even more important, running will help you to become really fit for probably the first time in your adult life.

What Is Fitness?

Out of shape . . . unfit—what do these terms really mean? "Out of shape" can be taken literally, of course: it can mean bulges, flabby muscles, excess weight. It can mean feeling tired all the time, yet not being able to sleep well. It can mean getting out of breath easily and being irritable. But it can also mean—and this is the most important meaning—the possibility of a shortened life.

Physiologists recognize three different kinds of fitness. These are muscular, skeletal, and cardiovascular. Muscular fitness has to do with the tone and strength of your basic muscle groups. Calisthenics such as push-ups, leg lifts and sit-ups are designed to strengthen and tone your muscles, and thus lead to muscular fitness. The second kind of fitness, skeletal, has primarily to do with flexibility. Bending to touch your toes, stretching exercises, and yoga asanas promote this kind of fitness.

The third kind, cardiovascular, is by far the most important. It refers to the strength and health of your heart and blood vessels. And, unfortunately, it is the kind of fitness that most of us are least aware of, because it doesn't show—at least not directly.

If you have flabby muscles you can always wear long sleeves to cover up jello-like upper arms; you can even, as I used to do, wear a girdle to force a bulging tummy into line underneath knit clothes. If you're too heavy or stiff to bend over easily, you can squat down or just learn not to drop things, and you can wear smocks to cover up the girth. There are many cosmetic and coverup measures you can use to disguise poor muscle tone and stiffness. But there is no coverup or cosmetic treatment to hide the condition of the most important muscle in your body: your heart.

It's hard to get worked up about your heart, I know. After all, it doesn't show; it just keeps doing its job, day after day, week after week, with no upkeep to speak of. Maybe it'll give out someday, but not for a long time, and anyway, you've heard that women don't have to worry about heart attacks.

That is only partly true. Granted, women as a group have less risk of heart attacks up to the age of menopause, because we're protected by our hormones. But after middle age, women's risk approaches men's. Besides, a poorly conditioned heart leads to more troubles than the ultimate one of heart attack, and many of these ailments can start early in life. You may have read about atherosclerosis, or hardening of the arteries, a condition in which your blood vessels become daily and increasingly clogged with deposits until one day the whole system shuts down and you die of a heart attack or a stroke. Atherosclerosis is commonly thought of as an old person's disease, but the fact is that the early signs of this horrifying killer are being detected in today's American teen-agers! High blood pressure is also a disease of the cardiovascular system, and this too is being discovered in young people. In fact, it's estimated that twenty-seven million Americans have heart or blood-vessel disease. That's almost one-sixth of our entire population!

Despite all these alarming statistics, I admit that the dangers of circulatory disease can seem remote—unless you find that you actually have one of these conditions, as I did five years ago. But think about it this way: your heart, which is only about the size of a closed fist, pumps more than 3,000 gallons of blood thousands of miles every day. Hardly a job for an out-of-shape muscle.

How can you tell if your heart is out of shape? You could take a special stress test under the supervision of a doctor. In this test you exert yourself to exhaustion, while the doctor monitors your heartbeat. By measuring such things as your resting heart rate, maximum rate under stress, and recovery rate, the doctor can determine how fit your cardiovascular system is. But there is a much easier way to find out the condition of your heart: simply ask your body. Can you run for a bus without getting out of breath? Can you walk up two or more flights of stairs without your heart pounding? Can you engage in strenuous physical activity without tiring? More to the point, can you run a mile and a quarter in twelve minutes or less? Can you walk two miles in half an hour? (*Don't* try these last two without your doctor's advice—but you probably know the answer already.) If the answer to any of these question is *no*, then your heart is not in good condition.

Fortunately, all muscles can be restored to good condition by the right kind of exercise. And this includes your heart. But what is the best way to exercise your heart?

As you know if you've ever taken a yoga or calisthenics class, enough activity of any sort will tone the muscles you are actually using. When I was a teen-ager, my best girlfriend could out-arm-wrestle most of the boys in our high school because her right forearm had become strong from brushing her waist-length hair a hundred strokes a day. And anyone who bowls, plays tennis, or carries a baby around knows that the muscles actually involved in the activity tend to become stronger and firmer. Each of these activities is actually a form of exercise.

All exercises—those we do as part of a class or those we do in the course of our daily lives—can be divided into two kinds: aerobic and anaerobic. What aerobic means, literally, is "promoting the supply and use of oxygen." You know you can't live without oxygen, but you may not know why. It's because activity of any sort—from balancing a checkbook to making love—uses energy. You get energy by burning fuel, which you take in the form of food. And the substance by means of which the fuel actually "burns" is oxygen.

Just as you can store fuel in a car by filling your tank with gasoline, so your body can store fuel—as it readily does, in the form of fat. But since there's no way to store oxygen, you have to keep taking it in continuously, by breathing. The better the supply of oxygen you have, and the more efficiently it can be delivered, the better your body can burn fuel and the more energy you will have.

Aerobic exercises, then, are those activities which improve your ability to take in and deliver oxygen to your body tissues. In aerobic exercises, you breathe hard and deep over a sustained period of time; your heart beats faster than normal for the same period; and you sweat a lot. The four basic aerobic exercises are running, walking, bicycling, and swimming.

All other exercises are basically anaerobic—they build muscle strength or improve flexibility, but do nothing to improve your ability to use oxygen. Weightlifting, stretching, yoga asanas, isometrics (exercises in which one muscle is pitted against another) are all anaerobic. To be sure, there are some sports, such as handball and tennis, which both build strength and tend to be aerobic. But these are usually not so sustained as the basic four, and only a sustained aerobic exercise can improve the condition of your heart, lungs, and circulatory system.

What Aerobics Can Do for You

How do aerobic exercises work? The sustained period of time spent on the exercise is the key—for during this time your heart is forced to work hard, and like any other muscle that works hard, it begins to improve its strength and tone. But that's only the beginning.

As you continue with an aerobics program, you will find it easier to breathe, both during and after the activity, because the muscles in your chest will have grown stronger from increased use; in addition, the capacity of your lungs may increase. When you have to do strenuous, tiring work, it will seem easier because you will be able to breathe more efficiently.

Your pulse rate will go down. As your heart becomes stronger and more efficient, it will be able to deliver more oxygen-carrying blood with each stroke, so it will need to beat fewer total strokes and will be able to rest longer between strokes.

The number and size of the blood vessels in your body will actually increase—as will the count of red cells in your blood. Not only will this help every cell of your body get more oxygen more quickly, but the increased flexibility and size of your blood vessels will help prevent some of the dangers of hardening of the arteries and high blood pressure.

But the benefits of aerobic exercise do not stop with the heart, lungs, and circulatory system. As you become healthier and more fit inside, these hidden benefits will be reflected on the outside—in the way you look and the way you feel. Increasing the supply of oxygen to your body tissues means that *all* these tissues will tend to become healthier. The muscle tone all over your body will improve. Your skin will become clearer. Your posture will improve. The vigorous exercise you are doing will burn calories. Even if you don't cut down on eating, you will tend to lose weight—and the weight you are carrying will be less evident, as flabby fat is replaced with firm muscle and redistributed. After a few months you will probably find that the shape of your body is becoming closer to the ideal for you.

You will also feel better all over. You'll be more relaxed and better able to sleep, but at the same time you'll have more energy for anything you want to do. Your capacity for doing anaerobic exercises—from sports to calisthenics to sex—will improve dramatically.

You can experience all of these psychological and physical benefits—and more—if you begin and stick with an aerobic exercise program. And the easiest and pleasantest of all the aerobic exercises, particularly for women, is running.

Why is running the ideal exercise for women? Well, let's take a brief look at the other aerobic exercises.

1. *Walking.* This exercise, humanity's oldest, has long been recognized as one of the best basic exercises. It can certainly be combined with a running program, and, as you will see, it forms the basis of any conditioning program. The main problem with walking is that it takes a long time to get aerobic benefits. You would have to walk as far as fifteen miles a week to get the benefits of running just one-quarter of that distance. Once you start running, though, you will find that you can walk longer and farther, and you will enjoy walking more. In my experience, even short walks used to be an ordeal. Painful, tired feet were an accepted fact of my life. But since I started running, all that has changed. I find that I can walk farther and faster, and that my feet *never* hurt. And sometimes, on days when I don't feel like running in the park or just don't have the time, I simply walk home from work to supplement my running program.

2. *Swimming.* Swimming is, as everyone knows, an excellent exercise for your whole body. But it's not a terribly practical one for most women on a day-to-day basis. To begin with, you have to know how to swim. Then you need to find something larger than a bathtub to swim in, such as a pool, a lake, or the ocean. You need good

weather—or access to an indoor pool. If you really like swimming, by all means swim. Like walking, swimming can be a good supplement to a running program. But remember that swimming involves exposing your eyes to chlorine or salt. You will most likely have to wash and dry your hair each time you swim. You have to have a clear area to swim in—just paddling around from side to side in a pool will not give you aerobic benefits—and you must swim continuously for at least fifteen minutes to begin to get the effects we've been talking about. That isn't always easy in a crowded pool or beach area.

3. *Bicycling*. Again, a terrific exercise, but it requires equipment. You need your bike, a lock, a chain, a place to keep the bike. Since aerobic exercises must be done for a sustained period of time, just riding your bike to work or around the neighborhood won't be of much benefit if you live in a city where stop-and-go traffic is common. Like walking and swimming, biking can be a supplemental part of your running program—and it can't be beat for recreation on a sunny Sunday afternoon. But once again, we come back to the fastest and easiest aerobic exercise:

4. *Running*. Running, for me and for millions of other American women, is the quickest, best, and easiest way to get the benefits of aerobic conditioning. Running requires no equipment other than a good pair of running shoes. Running can be done almost anywhere—out in the country, inside a gym, through city streets, in parks, along the beach. Running lets you feel the beneficial effects more quickly than the other aerobic exercises. Running doesn't require any particular coordination or even ability in sports, and after learning a few basic principles, almost anyone can do it well. Running can be done alone or with other people. Running can be fun, but even those times when it isn't—when it seems a chore—it's over with quickly. All you do is put on your running clothes, run, go home and shower—and you're through for the day. And running is an especially good exercise for women, because it is both a sport and an exercise you can keep up for the rest of your life.

According to *Runner's World* magazine, there are more than six million Americans who currently run, either competitively or for health. Most of these runners are men. Nobody knows just how many women are out on the roads, but from the results of competitive races and "fun runs," it is evident that the number of women runners of all ages is increasing rapidly.

Most women who take up running for health are not particularly interested in running races or in developing a set of muscles for the male-oriented sports we've never been given an opportunity to play. Since most of us just want to improve our fitness and appearance, running is the ideal exercise. Once you have become a runner, though, you may find that you will wish to join the growing number of women who race competitively. If so, you'll discover that your new sport is gaining acceptance all over the country, and that you will have a wide choice of races to enter, both mixed and for women only.

Although it is probably true that the best women runners will never be able to run as fast as the best men runners, some recent studies indicate that women may be able to run longer and farther than men. Now that women are starting to compete in ultramarathon running—which means running very long distances, fifty to one hundred miles or even more—it is being found that women may tire less quickly and have better all-round endurance than men.

You are probably not interested in running more than two or at most five miles, but isn't it nice to know that if you wanted to, you could (with proper training) probably outrun—in distance and length of time—any man you know?

Finally, running can be a lot of fun. That "camaraderie of the locker room" is just as satisfying to women as it is to men. This most rewarding aspect of my new life was brought home to me the last time my friend Fern and I went out running in the park together. We hadn't seen each other for a few weeks, so we ran slowly, talking, bringing each other up to date on jobs, lovers, life in general. Before we knew it we had run over four miles. Feeling tired and sweaty but really good, we went back to Fern's apartment and just sat around, drinking fruit juice and enjoying a profound sense of companionship and peace. We realized that the root of this companionship was our shared experience, that it had come from pushing ourselves to our physical limits together.

Fern suddenly smiled and said: "You know what? I really like being a jock."

Run or Jog?

I belong to two organizations: The National Jogging Association and Road Runners of America. In articles and books, you will often see the terms *running* and *jogging* used interchangeably. What's the difference? Technically, a jog is a slow run. All joggers are runners, but not all runners are joggers, or at least not all the time, though most runners jog sometimes.

The word *jogging* is also used to describe the kind of running we're talking about: running for health, regardless of how fast. Unfortunately, the word is sometimes used in a negative sense—it's what middle-aged men do to flatten their bellies, for instance. I personally think of myself as a runner, though I don't run fast and don't compete often or enjoy competition. But when I do run, as I do four times a week, I run as fast and as far as I can, and though my pace probably seems like a jog to the track star who passes me every other lap, *I* feel I am running, and therefore I consider myself a runner.

Whatever you call yourself, the important thing is to get out and do it.

3

Getting Started— What to Wear, Where and When to Run

"By nature, man is an animal made for running."—*Dr. Ernst van Aaken.*

By nature woman, too, is an animal made for running—but in our modern, complex world, few things are as simple as they should be. Even though running is the easiest, most natural, most hassle-free exercise you can take up, it will be even easier and more hassle-free if you take some time to prepare before you start. Following are detailed hints on shoes, dress, and times and places to run.

Shoes

By far the most important piece of equipment—the only thing, in fact, that you really *need*—is a good pair of running shoes. I can't emphasize that too strongly.

21

Why are special running shoes necessary? Bear in mind that each of your feet is composed of muscles, ligaments, and twenty-six fragile bones. Every step you take puts all your weight on those delicate feet. If you run a mile, each foot has to bear *all* your body weight more than two thousand times! It's only common sense that those feet should have the best support and protection you can possibly give them. And the only shoes that give them such support in the particular circumstance of running are shoes specifically designed and made *for* running.

If you already have a pair of tennis shoes, you probably don't see any reason why you can't run in them. After all, they're well made; they have an arch support and a non-slip rubber heel. I admit that when I started running, I too began with an old pair of tennis shoes, and every day I see a lot of people out on the track running in tennies. For an occasional five- or ten-minute run there is probably nothing wrong with tennis shoes. As far as that goes, you can run for the bus in a pair of high heels or platforms, though you certainly wouldn't want to make a practice of it. But remember, you are about to start a lifelong program of running for fun and health—not just an occasional run once or twice a month when the mood hits you. And for this, tennis shoes simply aren't good enough. Tennis shoes are, obviously, made for playing tennis. They are designed to help you keep your balance on the court, stop quickly and pivot on your toes, not run one to two miles on a track. Tennis shoes lack most of the basic features that are important in good running shoes, such as an elevated heel to prevent injuries of the calf muscles and the Achilles tendon (the tough cord that attaches your calf muscle to your heel).

If you're just going to try this program out—run for three weeks, say, to see how it feels—then maybe you should start with the tennis shoes you have. But if you seriously intend to stick with a running program, or even become a dedicated runner, then go out and buy a good pair of running shoes. They cost less than a good pair of imported sandals, and they'll save you time, money and trouble in the long run.

How to choose a pair of shoes

Buying a pair of running shoes is getting easier all the time, but it's still more difficult for women than for men. In the first place, the majority of manufacturers still make running shoes in men's sizes only. In the second place, most running shoes come in one width only: wide. The theory behind this unhappy fact seems to be that you can simply lace big shoes tightly enough to fit any foot. This may work with men's feet, but it can cause a real problem for women who have very narrow feet.

Fortunately, this situation is changing. Every year new companies come out with a line of running shoes, and the older, more established companies are beginning to recognize that a growing number of women runners want shoes of their own. But so far, most sporting-goods stores still don't carry women's running shoes in stock, so it is helpful to know how to figure your size in a man's shoe.

In general, you can estimate that your size in a man's shoe is your own size in a woman's shoe minus 1½ or 2. In other words, if you wear a size 10 woman's (as I do), then your man's size is probably 8 or 8½. But always try on the man's shoe. Just as with women's shoes, men's shoes can vary in size, depending on the cut of the particular model.

If your foot is wide, you will probably get a very good fit once you determine what man's size you wear. If you have a narrow foot, you may have to try on several pairs to find a style that is comfortable. Sometimes the problem of width can be solved by wearing two—or even more—pairs of socks while you are running. If your foot is very small or very narrow, and you simply can't get a man's shoe to fit you, then try boys' sizes. Fortunately, running shoes are a true unisex item, so no one will ever know (or care) that you're wearing men's shoes.

Where should you go to buy these men's (or possibly women's) shoes? Surprisingly, you can't buy running shoes in most shoe stores; you must go to a sporting-goods store, and even there you may find the selection of sizes, styles and brands quite limited. Some Y's and gyms sell sports equipment, including shoes, but the selection in this kind of small-service store is likely to be even narrower. An alternative to finding a store is to read the ads in sports magazines, such as *Runner's World,* and order shoes by mail. Some companies ask you to include a foot tracing, to make certain that you get a perfect fit.

A last alternative for women who don't live near a sporting-goods store is to go to a large chain shoe or department store. Many of these companies are now making their own lines of running shoes, though the quality of most of these shoes has still not been tested by large numbers of runners. A shoe may look exactly like a top-line shoe down to the last racing stripe yet lack some of the most important features of construction and material, so be very sure you know what to look for in this most important purchase. A bargain isn't a bargain if it causes you an injury—or worse, makes running so uncomfortable that you give it up.

Wherever you decide to buy your shoes, you should ask for general-purpose running shoes, also known as "training" shoes. These are sturdy shoes that will stand up to miles and miles of running, while giving your feet good suppport. Many training shoes are also used for racing, but racing shoes as such are lighter in weight than training shoes, and not always so durable.

These are the most important features to look for in any pair of running shoes:

1. *Layered sole.* This is very important, as a thick sole not only protects your foot but helps to absorb the body-jarring impact when your foot strikes the ground. The shoe you choose should have a layered sole thick from heel to toe. It should be thickest at the heel, but there should be at least one-half inch of cushioning under the ball of the foot. The sole should be of at least two layers: an inner, soft layer to cushion the foot, and an outer, tough layer to absorb shocks. You can see these layers when you look at the shoe from the side. If you are in doubt about the sole of a particular shoe, ask the salesper-

son who is helping you—or compare the shoe with photographs of a brand-name running shoe.

2. *Elevated heel*. This feature is important to all runners, but especially to women runners. Did you ever stop to think about the effect that years of wearing high-heel shoes have had on you? Well, aside from making you look taller and improving your sense of balance, high heels on shoes also contribute to a shortening of your calf muscles and Achilles tendon. Men also have this problem, just from wearing street shoes, but not to the same degree as most women. To compensate for this distortion of our natural build, running shoes are made with an elevated, lifted heel. Runners who are especially liable to Achilles-tendon and calf injuries sometimes add extra inside lifts to their shoes to further relieve strain on this area. You can check the elevation of a running shoe just by looking at the sole from the side. If the heel contains a wedge that makes it higher than the rest of the shoe by one-fourth to one-half inch, then it is adequately elevated. Many modern running shoes also have a rounded heel-lift at the back, which further helps prevent stress on the Achilles tendon.

3. *Flexibility*. To understand just how important this feature is, take off your shoes. Now walk around the room. Pay close attention to your feet. You'll notice that they bend, particularly where your toes

meet the ball of your foot, when you are about to "take off" to another step. When you're running, that bending at the toe area is dramatically exaggerated, so you want a shoe that will bend with your foot. If the shoe is too stiff, then your foot can't bend naturally, and the resultant stress can lead to foot and leg injuries. To test the flexibility of a running shoe, hold it by the heel with one hand, then press up on the toe with the fingers of your other hand. By applying only a little pressure, you should be able to bend the shoe up at a 90-degree angle at the ball of the foot. If the shoe does not bend easily, look for a different brand or model.

4. *Heel support*. This is a rigid support which covers the back part of the shoe and is designed to stabilize your heel while you run. It protects your foot and ankle from excess strain. You can tell if a shoe you are interested in has a heel support simply by feeling along the back of the heel. Then squeeze. Is the heel more rigid than the rest of the shoe? Most running shoes made today have a heel support.

5. *Arch support*. Podiatrists disagree on just how important this feature is, but most shoes have at least a minimal arch support. Many long-distance runners remove the built-in support and insert a specially constructed one of their own. You can tell if a shoe you are interested in has an arch support by looking inside the shoe. Then try on the shoe to see whether it is comfortable.

6. *Material*. Almost all running shoes are made of leather, or of nylon with leather inserts. There is very little difference in comfort in the two materials when the shoes are new. But after a while, leather tends to get stiff and crack, and so can cause blisters. Suede running shoes keep their flexibility longer than shiny leather ones, though eventually even suede will dry out. Nylon shoes are usually more lightweight and slightly more expensive than leather models. The cheapest shoes of all are made of vinyl, but these should be avoided, because they don't allow your foot to "breathe" and because their stiffness can cause blisters.

7. *Style*. Most modern running shoes tend to look alike; the only real differences are in color and the arrangement of stripes. Most models come in one color only, and the colors for all models are

pretty much limited to red, white, blue, yellow, and poisonous green. If your favorite color is purple, then you're out of luck—though I often run in my purple leotard and chartreuse running shoes and just ignore unkind comments. Kathy Switzer, one of the top distance runners in the country, simply buys color-coordinated hair ribbons; when she wears *her* poisonous green Adidas, she has matching poisonous green bows in her hair, and she looks smashing!

8. *Price*. The price of running shoes varies from just under twenty dollars to over forty. Most good shoes are somewhere in the twenty-to-thirty-dollar range. Sometimes you can save money by reading ads in sports magazines and buying factory seconds or by watching for sales. I realize that twenty to thirty dollars is a real investment, but remember: it's the *only* investment you have to make as far as your running goes. Any other money you put out is strictly optional. Then, too, a good pair of running shoes will last you a very long time. I still have the first pair of running shoes I ever bought, and I run in them sometimes, though my newer shoes are more comfortable and in better shape. If you buy good shoes to begin with and take reasonably good care of them, there's no reason why a pair won't last you two or more years.

Care of running shoes

If you want your new running shoes to last longer, you can buy special sole-protecting agents in sports stores or shoe-repair shops. These substances are designed to make shoes last longer by minimizing wear on the outer layer of the sole. Apply a sole protector when you notice the heel area of your shoe starting to wear down. Apply only a little, and spread it very thin and as smoothly as possible—no more than the original thickness of the sole. Another way to make shoes last longer is to send them to one of the companies that specialize in resoling athletic shoes. You can find ads for these companies in most sports magazines.

Remember that your running shoes are designed for running, not for walking around the city or playing tennis or volleyball. Avoid using your shoes for these purposes, and they will last a lot longer. Tennis and other racquet sports are especially hard on running shoes, because they require you to run on your toes and to twist and turn suddenly. Running shoes are not made for this kind of wear and will quickly develop holes in the toe area of the sole when used for these types of sports.

As for cleaning your running shoes, most of the runners I know don't bother doing it often. If your shoes are leather, occasionally wipe them clean with a good leather cream or saddle soap—it's not really necessary to polish them as you would street shoes. Nylon shoes can be scrubbed clean with a vegetable brush and a mild detergent.

If you follow all the tips in this section, you can be reasonably sure of getting a good, well-fitting pair of running shoes. The most popular well-known makers of shoes, in alphabetical order, are Adidas, Brooks, Karhu, New Balance, Nike, Patrick, Puma, Sports International, and Tiger. The only company that currently manufactures shoes in all widths is New Balance, though some Brooks models come in narrow, medium, and wide. Adidas, Brooks, and Saucony make some shoe models in women's sizes; in addition, Adidas makes a wide variety of children's running shoes. For the addresses of these and other companies that make good-quality running shoes, see the appendix.

What about running barefoot?

I'm sure you've seen children happily running through the grass in their bare feet, and from old jungle movies on TV we all know that primitive peoples run effortlessly through the forests either barefooted or in only the thinnest of moccasins. Well, if our feet could stay as young as children's, or if we lived in the pristine jungle, we could probably run barefoot too. But years of wearing street shoes, high heels and platform shoes, of walking on concrete and asphalt, of standing in lines while carrying heavy bags, of climbing stairs, of wearing poorly fitting shoes, have caused a lot of strain on our feet, our tendons, and our leg muscles. The fact is that most

modern Americans simply can't run safely in bare feet. The stresses
of civilization have taken too great a toll, and properly fitting running
shoes are the only way to compensate adequately for all those
stresses.

Even if your feet and legs are in perfect shape, it's still not a good
idea to run barefoot. There may not have been shoes in the Garden of
Eden, but a lot of other things weren't there either—broken glass,
dog dirt, concrete, bottle caps, rough asphalt, jagged potholes, and
rusty nails. It can be dangerous to walk around barefoot, let alone
run. And the dangers are everywhere. I have a friend who spent a lot
of time doing exercises to stretch his calf muscles so that he would be
able to run barefoot, "the way nature intended" him to run. For two
years he ran a few miles a week on a lovely grassy track in Santa
Monica, reporting rapturously on the sensual back-to-nature feeling
of soft grass beneath his bare feet. And then one day he stepped on a
hidden sprinkler head and gashed his foot so badly that he couldn't
run at all for three months.

The only place where I would recommend running barefoot is
along the beach. Again, it is probably better for you to run with shoes
on—and certainly safer, since you never know what you will find on a
beach these days. But most runners I know who run on the beach
don't like to get their shoes wet and then spend a lot of time drying
them out, and as a person who occasionally runs barefoot in the
sand, I can report that it is an almost mystical experience. I also have
to admit that it looks pretty silly to wear a sexy bikini with sweat
socks and red-and-white-striped training shoes.

What to Wear

The good news is that you can wear just about anything you wish
when you run. There are certain commonsense rules, of course—you
want to be comfortable, and presumably you want to look as good as
possible. But you can easily put together a running outfit from
clothes that you have right now in your drawers and closets; an outfit
that will look good, will be practical, and won't cost you a cent. (On

the other hand, you can spend hundreds of dollars on warm-up suits and monogrammed T-shirts if that's what you want.)

These are the things to think about when you're choosing a running costume. The most important consideration is that the clothes be loose, with no binding straps or belts, and nothing that will rub once you are in motion (or you can end up with nasty blisters in all sorts of unlikely places). In addition, the clothes should be absorbent, because you will be sweating a lot.

Other considerations are strictly a matter of individual choice. If you plan to carry keys or money with you, then pockets may be important. I usually pin a dollar or two inside my running shorts where it won't rub, and I either carry my keys in my hand or leave them in my mailbox. The fewer things you carry with you the better—a bulging pocket can be very uncomfortable after you have run for a few minutes. Sometimes I also carry an index card and a tiny pencil—again, usually pinned to my clothes—for jotting down the many brilliant ideas (or shopping lists) that come to me while I am actually on the track.

I usually don't worry too much about how I look when I'm out running, but I have friends who always look stunning; they wear nothing but chic T-shirts and expensive warm-up suits. One friend takes the opposite approach; she makes a point of wearing sweat suits and men's boxer shorts. "I'm a runner," she says, "and I want to look like one."

The best all-round fabric for running clothes is, not surprisingly, cotton, because it is lightweight and absorbent. Most experts advise you to avoid nylon and other synthetics, particularly in the summer, because these fabrics tend to get wet and clammy and don't have the insulating properties of cotton. But again, this is largely a matter of your individual preference.

Indoors or outdoors, summer and winter

You can wear the same clothes for running indoors or outdoors, but remember that indoor tracks tend to be located in hot and steamy gyms, so you should dress pretty much as you would for summer running. I sometimes see runners on my local indoor track wearing heavy sweat suits, and I inwardly shudder, though I know some runners don't feel they're really exercising unless they sweat profusely.

In the summer you can wear just about anything that's comfortable—most runners I know wear shorts as soon as the weather permits it, for comfort and a head start on tan legs, though some wear sweats or long pants all year. Some runners also add sunglasses and a sun hat, though I personally don't like to run with glasses on. If you do wear sunglasses (or regular glasses) you might attach an elastic to the back of the earpieces to keep the glasses from sliding down your nose as you run.

In winter, a little more care is necessary. When the thermometer says it's ten degrees above zero outside, you may be tempted to put on a heavy Shetland wool sweater and your suede overcoat, but resist the temptation. The best way to dress for running in winter is in layers—as many layers as necessary to keep you warm. Avoid bulk, because bulk will make it hard for you to bend and stretch. When you wear many layers of lightweight clothing, air becomes trapped between the layers and acts as a natural insulation to keep you warm. As you run you will warm up, and if you get too warm you can begin to shed the clothes, layer by layer. If you are running on a track, you can drop these clothes to the side, on the ground, to pick up later; if this is impractical, simply tie them around your waist. Though this may be a little inconvenient, it's much more comfortable than trying to deal with a heavy jacket once you have warmed up.

For a very cold day, the following would be a good running outfit: start with thermal underwear, or a long-sleeved cotton T-shirt and tights or hip socks; add two or more cotton turtleneck shirts; a sweat shirt or two; sweat pants or warm-up pants; two pairs of socks; a wool ski mask or hat; mittens or another pair of socks for your hands; and over all a zippered cotton jacket or—if it is damp—a nylon rain jacket.

Following are more specific suggestions on running clothes.

Leotards

If I had to choose my favorite all-round outfit for running, it would be leotards. The women runners I know agree with me by and large—I would say the leotard is the single most commonly worn item of running apparel next to running shoes.

Why are leotards so good for running? For one thing, since they are designed for dancers, they move and stretch with your body without tearing or slipping. They also look good—leotards come in just about every color, shade, and style that you can imagine, and because they are elastic they help to smooth out any unwelcome bulges you may have. Leotards can be worn with other things when you have finished running: they look fine with skirts, jeans, or by themselves at the beach. They rinse out easily and dry overnight.

When you buy a leotard, make sure that it fits. It should be fairly snug but not bind at the shoulder or in the crotch. I've found that the more expensive leotards fit better, bind less, and last longer than the cheaper brands.

Many women runners run in leotards and leotard tights with a long T-shirt over the leotard. This is a pretty sexy costume—the tights make your legs look long, firm, and slim—and the T-shirt can easily be lifted up to wipe sweat off your face. I prefer to run in a leotard with a pair of running shorts, and without tights, because tights make my legs feel sweaty and itchy. But experiment and find out what feels right for you. Because leotards come in so many styles, they can be worn all year round—a tank top in the heat of summer, long-sleeved in winter, and cap-sleeved for in between or running indoors.

T-shirts

Since they became a high-fashion item, T-shirts are not as inexpensive as they once were, though you can still find bargains if you look. Like many of my friends, I collect tees with different things printed on them, and I know it can be fun to have many different T-shirts in bright colors and with interesting logos to run in. A tee for running should be loose and absorbent. The only real caution here is that some imported cotton T-shirts aren't color-fast, so when you start sweating the color may run.

Shorts

You probably have around the house somewhere an old pair of tennis shorts which would be perfect to run in. In any pair of running shorts, the waist should be loose—either lightly elasticized or buttoned, and without a belt, which is most uncomfortable to run in. If your shorts have a zipper, make sure it is in good working order, because zippers have a way of coming unzipped during the course of a run. Most important of all, the shorts should *not* be tight in the legs or binding at the crotch, because they might wear blisters on the insides of your thighs.

Cutoff jeans are generally not good for running in because they tend to be stiff and rub at the waist and on the insides of your thighs. If you do wear cutoffs, make sure that the denim is old and very soft, and don't roll up the cuffs. If rubbing is a problem, try slitting the legs an inch or so at the side seam.

The best (if the ugliest) running shorts are boxer-style gym shorts, which are made for active sports. These have a loosely elasticized waist, wide legs, and no zipper—and also usually no pockets, which may be a drawback. Another drawback is that you can buy this kind of shorts only in a sporting-goods store or in the men's department of a department store. You can find similar shorts made for women in the tennis department, but usually at three times the cost. The first time I tried to buy boxer shorts I got no help at all from the salesman:

"May I help you?"

"I want to buy a pair of running shorts."

"Fine. Is it for your husband?"

"For me."

"Oh. What size are you?"

"Well, I don't know. These are men's sizes. I'd have to try them on."

"I'm sorry, we don't have a fitting room in this department."

"But I don't know what size I am."

"Well, what size pants do you wear?"

"You mean in *men's* sizes?"

I finally chose a pair of mediums, more or less at random, and when I got them home I found that they fit just fine.

Underwear

I have a friend who never wears underpants in any circumstances at all, including when she runs, but most women runners do wear undies, usually of cotton, to absorb sweat. The only real caution here is that you should be careful if you wear bikini panties—they are often tightly elasticized in the legs and can become very uncomfortable when you are running.

To the question of whether to wear a bra while you run, there is no definitive answer. Some doctors say that you must *always* wear one when you run or you will break down the tendons and tissues of your breasts. Other doctors say there is no scientific evidence that running affects your breasts one way or another. You might ask your own doctor before you begin running, but chances are he or she will say yes, just to be safe.

The women runners I have questioned are divided on the matter. Most do wear bras when they run, but others never do. Many of those who don't wear a bra wear some other supportive garment: a tight leotard or a tank-top bathing suit are among the most popular items. I prefer not to wear a bra when I run, and usually wear a tight leotard instead—but here again it's a matter of what you prefer and what feels most comfortable.

The women who don't wear bras tend to have smaller breasts than those who always wear them—one woman with very large breasts not only wears a bra but also ties a large silk scarf around her chest because she can't stand the feeling of bouncing while she runs.

Certainly you will hear fewer obscene comments on the streets if you wear some support to prevent bouncing, and if you are like most women you will probably find that it's more comfortable to wear a bra around the time of your menstrual period.

If you don't like to wear a bra at all, ever, you will probably discover after a few weeks of running that your breasts are noticeably firmer, so you will look better bra-less in street clothes.

Socks

Some women (and men) run without socks, but this isn't generally a good idea. Socks serve two functions: they protect your feet from rubbing against the leather or nylon of your running shoes (and blistering), and they absorb sweat, which further protects your feet and also helps keep your shoes from deteriorating.

Cotton socks are the best kind, because they are so absorbent, though nylon socks may protect slightly better against rubbing. In winter you may prefer wool socks for warmth, or a pair of cotton socks underneath wool socks. The three main types of athletic socks are the anklet type, or women's tennis socks, tube socks, and cushioned athletic socks. Anklet socks cover only your foot, just up to the rim of the shoe: they are classier looking than men's style socks, but may not be as thick or afford as much protection. This type of sock usually has a tassel of some sort at the back to keep the sock from slipping down inside your shoe. Tube socks are just what the name implies: a long tube, with no shaping at the toe or heel. These are usually very inexpensive and stay up well while you are running. Cushioned athletic socks are formed at the heel and toe and are lined in the foot part with terry cloth. These are the most comfortable socks to wear, because they provide the cushioning of two pairs of socks without the bulk, but they usually come only in men's sizes and are much more expensive than the other types of athletic socks.

If you want to just wear some socks that you have around the house, that's okay too—one of my friends often runs in patterned knee socks. The important thing is that the socks you are wearing should be neither too loose nor too tight.

Warm-up outfits, sweats, jeans

So far I've been talking about all-weather running clothes. Many runners wear shorts even in winter. But when the weather gets brisk you'll probably want to cover up a little more. Again, you can make do with clothes you already have around the house, but when it starts to get really cold, I would advise you to buy a pair of sweat pants, which are shapeless trousers made of cotton sweat-shirt material. Most sweats have elastic at the ankles and tie with a drawstring at the waist. They are quite inexpensive, around five dollars or less in sporting-goods stores, and usually come in blue or gray. The reason sweat pants are so good for running is that they are very absorbent and completely nonbinding. The thick material keeps your legs warm in winter, but because sweats fit so loosely, they are comfortable in warmer weather too.

The drawbacks to sweat pants are that they are ugly and shapeless and usually don't come with pockets. Also, a new pair of sweat pants sheds on the inside, so you will have little pills of cotton fuzz all over your legs and the floor until the pants have been washed two or three times.

If you don't want to get a pair of sweat pants, the next best thing is a loose-fitting pair of blue jeans, preferably a pair that has been washed to the point of softness. New jeans are much too stiff and will rub in the waist and at the crotch. They don't have much give, and so are uncomfortable to do warm-up exercises in. If your jeans are fashionably long, then be sure to roll them up at the ankle before you start running, or you could trip.

The best kind of running jacket is a sweat-shirt jacket with a hood and zipper. These cotton jackets, which cost under ten dollars, are very warm and lightweight, and are my favorites, after leotards, for all-round running clothes. Most sweat jackets come with wide pockets, which you can pin shut. They are warm enough for running in very cold weather, but if you get too hot during a run, it's easy to unzip a sweat jacket and tie it around your waist. These jackets wash easily, can be put in the dryer, and look good with jeans.

Regular sweat shirts, the kind that pull over your head, are also good for running in cold weather, for the same reasons as sweat-shirt jackets. They cost somewhat less, but are not so versatile as the jacket type.

Coordinated warm-up suits

I admit they look pretty good, those brightly colored, striped, fitted synthetic or cotton suits. A friend who has one wouldn't dream of running in anything else, because, as she puts it, "Once I have on my warm-up suit I really feel and look like a runner, so what else can I do but run?"

Warm-up suits come in a variety of colors. Most have pockets; some have hoods. They can cost anywhere from fifteen dollars to fifty or more, with the average around thirty dollars. I have never owned one, mainly because it seems silly to spend that kind of money for clothing to go out and get sweaty in, but if you want to get one, watch for sales. These suits too wash and dry easily.

Rubber sweats

These are sweat pants and jackets made of rubber for people who want to sweat a lot while exercising. NEVER wear rubber sweats while running! These outfits are designed for less vigorous activity, and if you run in one you could become overheated and suffer heat stroke.

Hair—hats—sweat bands

What to do about your hair is an important consideration in running. I wear my hair very short, so I just wash it when I shower after running. But when I started running I had long hair and found I was much more comfortable if I pinned it up or braided it. Most women runners with long hair at least tie their hair back, because it can be annoying to have it swinging in your face; also, very long hair will make you feel sweatier around the neck and head.

If you don't like the feeling of sweat dripping down your face or on your neck, you might try wearing a sweat band, which can also help hold your hair back. You can buy these for one to two dollars at a sporting-goods store. Or make your own: take an old towel or piece of terry cloth and cut a long strip, two to three inches wide, then fold it in half the long way. Put the sweat band around your forehead and tie it in back.

Some women runners wear bandanas to catch sweat and help control their hair. You can buy the brightly printed cowboy-type cotton ones in any variety store. They come in all colors and can be color-matched to leotards for a coordinated look.

If you decide to wear your hair up for running, be sure it is pinned or barretted very securely, because the action of running will tend to cause hair and pins to work loose, and you may find yourself with hair in your face while you shed bobby pins all over the track.

Many runners like to wear hats while running in the summer sun. Aside from protecting your face from too much sun, hats can also help control sweating. The best kind to get are terry cloth or plain cotton tennis hats. You want something very lightweight, with a brim, and washable. You can also buy a visor rim that ties around the head. Women with very long hair may find this kind of hat more comfortable, as it leaves room for you to pile and fasten your hair on top of your head.

Other accessories

There's no reason not to wear jewelry while you run, but be careful about certain things. If you wear screw-type earrings, it's best to remove them before running because they can work loose and get lost during the run. If you have pierced ears, losing earrings isn't a problem, but heavy earrings which bounce can make your earlobes sore after a while.

As for necklaces and bracelets, it's up to you, but I once lost one of my favorite thin chains when the clasp somehow worked loose during a three-mile run. Some women notice a temporary swelling of their hands and fingers during and just after running, so tight rings might become uncomfortable.

What about a watch? You will probably want to wear one, at least at first, so you can keep track of your time and speed. Be sure that your watchband isn't tight—I once found my hand growing numb from a new and too-tight watchband. If your watchband is uncomfortable, try pinning your watch to your clothing or carrying it in your hand.

There's no need to buy a stopwatch unless you want to, because the *exact* time you run isn't really important. I decided to buy a stopwatch after I had been running for two years so I could find out how long it took me to run one mile as fast as I could. I went out and ran that one mile—then put the expensive watch away in a drawer and haven't used it since.

Another piece of optional equipment you may want to buy is a lap counter, a small stainless-steel device that you carry in your hand as you run to keep track of the number of laps you have run. This is most useful if you plan to do most of your running on a small indoor track with several laps to the mile. A lap counter costs around six to ten dollars and can be bought in any sporting-goods store.

All other dress considerations, including make-up and perfume, are strictly up to you. As far as one man I know is concerned, any woman looks good running, "because I know she really cares about herself, and is doing something to take care of her body."

Care of running clothes

Whether you go out and buy an expensive warm-up suit or just throw something together from the back of the closet, it is very important to keep your running clothes clean. Shirts, leotards, and socks which you run in more than once or twice will get stiff and unbelievably smelly if they aren't at least rinsed out. They will also wear out faster, especially socks.

Sweat suits and pants needn't be washed so often, but should be washed at least every couple of weeks. It's also a good idea to set aside a special place to keep your running clothes—a large drawer, say, or an area of your closet where they will have room to air out between runs.

Where to Run

You can run anywhere. Literally. Indoors or out, on a track or in the street. For most women, the problem isn't so much finding a place to run, but choosing from among the many possibilities.

Indoors

Possibly one of the easiest ways to get started is to run on an indoor track. These tracks are made of a resilient surface, such as the rubberized material known as "Tartan," and are usually built around an indoor gym. The track I sometimes run on is set above the basketball gym at my local YMCA and is approximately twenty-four laps to the mile. Advantages of these tracks, especially for beginners, are that there will be other beginners running, that you don't need to worry about weather, and that the pace on the track will be relatively slow. You also have the advantage of knowing exactly how long a distance one lap is.

To find an indoor track near you, check with your local YMCA, YWCA, or other gym. Some health clubs have indoor tracks, though most don't. Some gyms and Y's without tracks set aside an area around the gym (or perhaps around the swimming pool). The surface here is not so nice as Tartan, but a measured distance is marked off, and the area is reserved for runners.

Many health clubs that don't have room for a track maintain one or more "running machines," which can be set for various speeds and inclines. You can do all your running on such a machine if there is no other possibility, but they are very boring for most people to run on.

Finally, if you live in a large apartment building and can't find anywhere else to run, try running in the hall. Yes, the hall. One woman I know was forced indoors by three weeks of damp, muddy weather. Finally, in desperation, she paced off the carpeted hall in her large co-op building, discovered that from one end to the other was approximately 1/32 mile—and started running. "I got weird looks from the ladies in the laundry room," she reports, "but it was worth it to get back to my running."

Outdoors

I would like to insert a small commercial here for running outdoors. In my first year and a half of running, I ran exclusively on a small indoor track. When I finally ventured outside, I didn't like it—it seemed harder to run on a dirt track, and I found the variable weather conditions distracting. But once I got used to it, I came to love running outdoors, in all weather, and now I run inside only when I'm forced to—by a blizzard, say, or when I'm running late at night. If you live in a city, as I do, try to find a place to run outside. Even if you don't have access to a beautiful path along a river, I think you'll find the contact with open air and sky a refreshing and invigorating change from walls, fluorescent lights, and that closed-in feeling.

Your choice of where to run outdoors really depends on your philosophy: I like to know how *far* I am running, but many other women prefer to know how *long* they have run. Regardless of your preference, it is probably easiest to start running on a track, if you can find one. The main reason for this is that on a track, you don't have to worry about dogs, potholes, cars, or uneven surfaces. But since track running (indoors or outdoors) is boring for some people, you may wish to alternate track running with "free running."

Where to find a track

Many cities have municipally maintained tracks in city parks— usually one-fourth mile or one-eighth mile long. New York City, for example, has several eighth-mile tracks in its parks as well as a 1.58-mile track around the reservoir in Central Park. After you have been running awhile, you will know the distance of a track just by looking at it, but if you are unsure at first, ask another runner. To find the municipal track nearest you, call your city department of parks and recreation.

If your city does not have municipal tracks, or if you live too far from one, check out the nearest junior high, high school, city college, or university. Most of these have tracks, usually quarter-mile tracks, and almost always these will be open to non-school runners. Call the school's physical education department to find out when the track is open to the public. Most tracks are open at all times except when an actual track meet is in progress, though some allow non-students only in the early morning and late afternoon hours. If the school says outsiders aren't allowed at any time, you might check it out anyway during off-hours. I can almost guarantee that at least in the early morning there will be some runners out there.

If you run exclusively on a track, it's important to alternate the direction in which you run. Since most tracks are banked, your outer leg tends to come down at a slightly different angle from your inner leg; also, because of the curvature of the track, your legs move through slightly different angles, and over a period of time this can cause problems. The indoor track at my local Y has a mandatory change from clockwise to counterclockwise every week. Unfortunately, most tracks are *always* run counterclockwise. If this is true at the track you use, try running clockwise on the grass on the inside of the track or on the extreme outside lane, at least once in a while.

How to measure a course

If you prefer not to run on a track or find it difficult to get to one, but still would rather run a measured distance, then your best bet is to mark out your own course. The easiest way to do this is to borrow or rent a bicycle with an odometer and ride over the course you want to run. Choose some landmark to start (for instance, a street sign if your course is along a street), then note landmarks at approximately quarter-mile intervals. Your course can be as long or as short as you wish; while you are still a beginner it might be easiest for you to mark

off a short distance—say one-quarter to one-half mile—and run/
walk back and forth on this course until you are ready for longer runs.

Another way to measure a course is to drive along it in a car,
though this obviously won't work on a trail in the country or in a city
park. The final alternative is to walk for a while on a measured track,
using a watch to determine your pace (say a twenty-minute mile),
then walk at that same pace over the course you wish to run. Five
minutes at a twenty-minute pace will give you approximately a
quarter mile, ten minutes a half mile, and so on.

It's important to know something about the surface you'll be
running on. The advantage of most tracks is that they are composed
of Tartan, dirt, cinders, or some other substance which tends to
cushion your feet while providing a good running surface. If you find
that you will be doing most of your running on concrete or asphalt, be
sure that your shoes are especially well cushioned, and wear two
pairs of socks to further protect your feet. Grass is nice to run
on—but long grass can hide holes, dog dirt, and other obstacles, so
be especially careful when you run on grass. Dirt or cinder trails can
become very uneven after a rain, but running in mud poses no
special problems other than getting your legs and running clothes
muddy.

In the city

Probably the best place for city running is along a trail in a park,
which will separate you from cars and exhaust fumes. Cities that
have lakes and rivers usually have walking and jogging paths
alongside the water.

If you can't find a track or path to run on, the next best place for
city dwellers to run is along the perimeter of a park. Some parks have
pedestrian or bike paths set back from the street, or you can run on
the grass, the sidewalk, or even in the road around the park. If you
run in the street, try to run *against* the direction of traffic, and wear
light-colored clothes if you are running at night. I have a friend who

sometimes runs in the street alongside Central Park in New York late at night. I once asked her if she was worried about muggers. "Are you kidding?" she said. "I don't carry anything worth stealing. What really worries me is buses. I think the city gives them points for running down joggers."

Thoughtless drivers can be a real problem for city-street runners, and your only real defense against them is to stay alert and be prepared to hit the side of the road if necessary.

If all else fails, you can just go out and run around your own block. In many cities, twenty blocks equals one mile, so if you run around your block five times (5 × 4 sides) you will have run one mile. Running around the block can be a good way to start a running program, and even if you usually run in a park or on a track, it can be a good alternative if you are pressed for time or want to run late at night. The main drawback to running on sidewalks is that you will have to schedule your running for off-hours, when most pedestrians and children are off the street.

Remember that aerobic exercise must be continuous to give you benefits; so if you do your running on the sidewalk or in the street, when you come to a red light either jog slowly in place or run around in small circles while waiting for the light to change.

Suburban and country running

Women who live in suburbs and who do not want to walk or drive to a track can also run on sidewalks or streets. The traffic is usually lighter there than in city streets, so your run will be more pleasant; since most suburban blocks are irregular in length, however, you will probably have to drive your course first to get an idea of the distance.

If you live in the country, you can run along any road or path in the woods or fields. Country running is especially pleasant because you can really feel at one with nature, and the air is usually purer than urban air. The main things to watch out for in the country are uneven surfaces and obstacles that might trip you.

Suburban and country runners share one other hazard that can make a runner's life miserable, and that is dogs. For some unknown reason, some pet dogs who ordinarily take seriously their role as man's best friend look upon runners as legitimate prey. Maybe they think you're delivering the mail. If the course you run is likely to have unfriendly dogs on it, most experts advise you to carry a stick or a can of dog repellent, the kind that mail carriers use. Sometimes just stopping your run works—it seems to turn you back into a recognizable human being in the dog's mind. If you find yourself seriously challenged by a dog and don't have any kind of repellent or weapon, bend down and pretend to pick up a rock. Most dogs understand this gesture and will back down. If the idea of being chased by dogs completely unnerves you, as it does me, then don't run alone in areas where you may feel threatened.

If you live near a beach, you have access to one of the best natural places to run. The surface is best just above the water line, where the sand is packed hard. Sand has no spring at all and absorbs most of your forward momentum, so you may find it somewhat harder to run on the beach than in other places—but there's something so spiritual about it as you run along, feeling the sea breeze and ocean spray, that it makes up for anything, even getting your sweat pants soaked.

If after all these suggestions you still think you don't have a place to run, or you can't find the best place in your neighborhood, then just go outside some morning between seven and nine, or some afternoon between five and seven, and look for runners. I can guarantee you'll see a few and probably several; wherever they are running is a place to run. Or ask a runner who is walking home. (Though most runners are friendly and happy to help beginners, it's not a good idea to try to strike up a conversation with someone in the middle of a run.) Ask that runner where and when she or he usually runs, and you'll probably find the most popular course in your neighborhood.

The point is, unless you want to be completely alone when you run, you won't be. Even fifteen years ago, the few runners you saw were considered health freaks; today there are so many people on the roads that runners have become almost a part of the landscape. I have seen people running at all hours in some of the most unlikely places (I once saw a man running at two A.M. in the garment district of New York, for example). Running feels so good that confirmed runners will go to any lengths to find a place to do it—and so will you, once you get started.

To give you an idea how easy it is to find a place to run, I recently spent six months in Santa Monica, California. These are some of the places that I ran: along the beach, barefoot; down the median strip of San Vicente Boulevard with dozens of other runners; on the outside lane of the wonderful, bouncy red track at UCLA, where the famous woman runner Francie Larrieu was working out on an inner lane; on the grass track along the inside of the athletic field of Santa Monica Community College, while Bruce Dern, the actor, worked out on the quarter-mile dirt track; and alone on the hilly streets of the neighborhood around the Santa Monica airport.

When to Run

Obviously, you can run any time of the day or night, but you should experiment to find the time that is best for you. Just as some people are night people and others are day people, some feel better running in the morning, others in the evening.

I know women who can't start the day unless they've had a morning run. "It wakes me up," says my friend Joyce. "My morning run gives me energy all day long."

I'm just the opposite. Even though I sometimes run in the morning, especially on weekends, I prefer to run in the late afternoon to early evening, after work. Since I spend a lot of time sitting at a desk, by the end of the day I usually feel (and probably look) like the female equivalent of Quasimodo. But after a few minutes on the track I start to feel my back straighten out, and all the tensions of the day just seem to melt away. For me, a late-afternoon run is better than taking a nap. No matter how tired, cranky and achy I feel, once I'm through running I'm full of new energy and ready to spend an evening full of exciting or even virtuous activities.

My friend Dick prefers to run at lunchtime. He started running in a program sponsored by his company for busy executives who wanted to lose weight. For six weeks the men were put through a program of running on a local track, and they ate only a very light lunch. After that time Dick was hooked, and I saw him change, over a few months, from a pot-bellied, stoop-shouldered nervous wreck to a taller, well-built, relaxed athlete. His wife too was so impressed that she started running at noon at the local Y. Since her program isn't company-sponsored, and since it takes her about an hour and a half to get to the Y, run, shower, and go back to work, she has to work a little later in the evening, but she feels it's worth it. "I feel so much better," she says. "I used to just sit around like a zombie waiting for quitting time. Now, after my run, I go back to work full of energy and ready to do whatever has to be done."

I have another friend who runs only late at night because she works till nine and doesn't like to run in the morning. For her, too, it's worth it, although she admits that it sometimes interferes with her social life.

Whatever time of day or night you decide to run, there are a few commonsense rules to follow. The most important of these is NEVER to run after eating. Most doctors advise you to wait *at least* two hours before running. I find I feel much better if I wait at least three hours or even longer if I've had more than a light meal. The time required for digestion varies with different people; experiment and find out what is right for you.

Some women make a point of running only on an empty stomach: only first thing in the morning, or in the evening, after having skipped lunch. Some marathoners have been known to run more than twenty-five miles after fasting for twenty-four hours (though this practice obviously isn't recommended). If you feel you must have something in your stomach to give you energy, try drinking a glass of juice before you run—but then wait at least fifteen minutes before going out.

Another important practice is to go to the bathroom before you run—and as close to the run as possible. There is nothing more uncomfortable than trying to run with a full bladder, and if your colon is full you may get a stomach ache after you've run for a few minutes. Fortunately, running is itself a great cure for constipation.

Nor is it a very good idea to run right after having sex, because at that time your body wants to relax rather than work. But it's a myth that an active sex life interferes with athletic performance. In fact, just the opposite seems to be true: you will probably find you have more energy for sex after you've been running for a few weeks.

If you are taking an exercise or dance class, try to schedule your running for after the class. The same applies if you do calisthenics on your own. Though opinion is somewhat divided, most experts feel that it is better to do exercises first, as a warm-up for running. On the other hand, if you take a yoga class, you should run first and go to the class afterwards. In other words, if the activity is in the nature of a warm-up, do it first; if the activity is relaxing, run first and use the activity to cool off.

Weather

The ideal temperature range for running is 40° to 70° Fahrenheit (4.5° to 21° Celsius). The cooler the temperature, though, the better. The most comfortable is probably between 40° and 60° Fahrenheit, with a slight breeze.

Surprisingly, heat causes many more problems for runners than cold. Unless you are planning to run in Siberia in the dead of winter, you can handle almost any degree of cold just by putting on more layers of clothes; the opposite is not true, though, in the summer. Whenever the temperature goes above eighty degrees, particularly if it is humid, be very careful. Go slower than your usual pace. Drink water before you run. (Yes, *before*—unlike taking in food, drinking water before running won't bother you, once you get used to feeling a sloshing in your stomach.) If it is very hot and you sweat profusely, drink plenty of fluids after you run as well. Fruit and vegetable juices are good, or you can buy one of the special beverages made for athletes.

Some runners have a tendency to rub heat blisters on the insides of their thighs during hot, humid weather. If this is a problem for you, first make sure that your shorts are loose and not rubbing there. Then put lots of powder on your thighs before you run. If that doesn't work, try oiling your thighs with Vaseline or baby oil. If you still have blisters, give up and switch to a pair of long pants of some very absorbent material.

Running in the sun is a good way to get an even tan, because you usually change direction often, but be as careful as you are when you go to the beach. If you want to protect your skin from premature wrinkling, use one of the anti-tan lotions which contain PABA (p-Amino Benzoic Acid). Apply it half an hour before you go out, but be very careful, because it stains clothing.

The final note about summer is an obvious one: try to schedule your running time for very early in the morning, or very late in the afternoon or even at night. My runner friends in Arizona usually run at night on a local high-school track before a late dinner.

As I mentioned in the section on clothing, you can handle cold most easily by adding layers of clothes. Most important, particularly on cold, windy days, is some sort of hat, because you lose sixty percent of your body heat through your head. Surprisingly, running in extreme cold isn't so unpleasant for most runners as running in the heat; in fact, it can sometimes be exhilarating. The only real hazard of winter running, particularly in cold climates, is the danger of losing your footing on an icy track or snowy trail. You probably wouldn't want to go out running in a snowstorm or on sub-zero days, though there are some runners who do; but if you have a place to run that is ice-free, there's no reason why you can't run throughout the entire winter.

Rain can be a more serious problem. If it doesn't rain often where you live, then just stay inside on damp days and think virtuous thoughts. If you live in a section of the country where it rains a great deal, like the Pacific Northwest, and you don't have access to an indoor track, your best bet is to buy a lightweight rubber rain poncho. It's never a good idea to wear sweats or any other thick materials in the rain, because they get soaked easily and become very heavy from the water. It's also—need I add?—very dangerous to go out running in a thunderstorm (though I've done it on occasion). Running in a light rain can actually be very pleasant, if it's warm, and I often find my local track crowded on wet spring days. Running while it's snowing can also be a lot of fun.

Wind is a problem only if it's very strong—as you know, a cold day feels much colder if there is a substantial wind-chill factor. Conversely, wind can make a hot, humid day a little more bearable, because it evaporates your sweat quickly. If it's extremely windy I usually stay indoors—running against a strong wind can be almost as difficult as running up a hill.

Now you know what to wear, where to run, and when. The next chapter will show you how and give you specific programs for starting. So—slip into your leotard and running shorts, put on your track shoes, go find a course, and get ready to begin.

4

How to Run

T HE title of this chapter has a double meaning. The first meaning is the one you are expecting: how to start a running program. The second meaning, and the one we're going to look at first, is literal: what are the actual mechanics of effortless, efficient running?

"I know how to run," you may be thinking. "Everyone does. It's as natural as . . . as . . . well, as running."

True. You almost certainly do know how to run; that is, you can put one foot more or less in front of the other at a fast enough pace to catch up to a friend across the street or to get that one vacant taxicab two blocks away at three in the morning. But you probably don't have the know-how to run efficiently and comfortably for any period of time. After all, why should you? The fact is that very few adult females in America today have the vaguest idea how to run in the sense we are talking about. This is not to imply that most men run correctly the first time they set foot on a track, but more men than women have at least been exposed to opportunities for running.

I owe my present style mostly to the kindness of other runners. During my first six weeks, for example, a fellow runner (male) pointed out one day that my feet did not move straight forward and back, but rather flew out to the side in back. This not only was inefficient, he added, but could put unusual stress on my knees—which had begun to be very sore, particularly when I was running. I thanked him for the advice and began to pay attention to what my feet were doing, and sure enough, they were flopping out at an awkward angle in the back. This is in fact one of the commonest faults of female runners. One reason for it is that we've never been taught to run properly; another is that many women tend to be somewhat knock-kneed, and so their feet do not move naturally as straight as they might wish.

Most of the other fine points of my running—which will never win any medals for style—have also come to me through the comments of other runners. Following are hints on the most important things to be aware of; read through these suggestions and try to incorporate them into your running as much as possible. Your goal is to keep the how-to's in mind without being consciously aware of them: as you run more and more you will find your style and comfort improving without any conscious effort on your part. I'm still working on my form—but let's hope that you'll start out on the right foot and stay there!

General Tips

The most important thing to remember about your running style is *to relax*. Running is not a precision activity, requiring one hundred percent of your concentration; rather, unless you are entering a race and hope to win it, running should be a chance to let your mind roam free and your body react as naturally and loosely as possible.

Your posture is just as important when you are running as at all

other times. Your body should be as straight as possible, and nearly erect, with a very slight tilt forward. Your shoulders should be held naturally, neither back nor forward, and your head should be up. As you come down on your feet, try not to bounce—in other words, run with as smooth a gait as possible. Coming down softly and smoothly takes a little bit of practice, but not much. Think soft.

What to Do with Your Feet

Many women start out running on their toes or on the balls of their feet, because they have seen other runners doing this or because it seems somehow natural (maybe because we're used to high heels). *Don't* run this way; it puts excessive strain on your foot itself as well as on the tendons and muscles of your legs and ankles. The safest and most comfortable way to run is *flatfooted*, or nearly so. If any part of the foot strikes the ground first, it should be your heel; then you should roll forward, slightly flexing your foot, until you "take off" from the ball of your foot to the next step.

Your feet themselves should move forward and back in as straight a line as possible, like the pendulum of a clock.

Legs

Another fault I had when I started running is one I notice often in beginning women runners: for some reason, we tend to shuffle when we run. Make a conscious effort, from the very first time you run, to lift your legs from the thigh. To get a feel for this kind of lifting, walk around the room, making an effort to raise your thighs to waist level with each step. The thighs themselves should be almost parallel to the ground in this exercise; in running, obviously, you will not lift them quite that high. Lifting from the thigh helps to develop your leg muscles and puts more power into your stride. If you want to run faster, just lift your legs higher.

And Arms

Arms? What do they have to do with running? Seemingly not much, but holding your arms incorrectly or moving them excessively can cause you to bounce too much. It can also cause your whole body to twist as you run, which cuts down on the speed and efficiency of your stride and can lead to fatigue and even muscle strain.

Where to carry your hands is also an important consideration. Many women tend to carry them high, near the shoulder. This not only is inefficient; it will tire you out very quickly. The best place to carry your hands is at about waist level. The arms should be bent so that your forearms are nearly parallel to the ground; when you stride forward, your forearms will be tilted slightly upward, and when you reach the end of your stride, your forearms will point slightly downward, toward the ground. As you run, you should let your arms swing naturally, forward and back, and parallel to each other. Try to keep them from swinging stiffly or out to the side.

Don't let your hands flop as you run; they should be natural extensions of your arms. You should carry them neither open nor closed, but loosely clenched. A common problem with many women runners (and men, too!) is a tendency to let the hands slowly clench into a fist until they are held tightly and almost angrily. This clenching not only keeps you from relaxing as you run but also prevents your arms from swinging naturally and thus can affect the rest of your stride. This is a problem that I have to work on constantly. I usually choose a few moments during my run—say, every six laps or so—to check my form, particularly in regard to relaxation. Are my shoulders tight? Are my hands clenched? More often than not, the answer is *yes*, and so I "shake out" for a few strides, letting my arms flop loosely as I move my shoulders forward and backward. Then I resume my normal stride and usually feel much more relaxed.

Some runners consciously pump their arms as they run, exaggerating the normal backward and forward motion. In addition to wasting energy, this can cause your back to become tense, thus destroying any hope of relaxation. The only time you should pump your arms is in the last stages of going up a hill; somehow the pumping action seems to make it easier to pull your tired body up those last few feet.

If you want to check your form after you've been running for a few weeks, try running with the sun at your back, and watch your shadow as it stretches out in front of you. While you won't be able to observe any fine points this way, you should be able to see whether your body is twisting unnecessarily, or whether you are bouncing instead of gliding smoothly along. Another way to check, if you are a track runner, is to count your paces on each lap for several laps; if your foot hits the ground about the same number of times within each lap, then you are probably running in a "groove" that is right for you. The final way to check your stride, of course, is to ask another runner to observe you as you run. Most runners will be happy to do this, and may be able to help you spot a bad habit you weren't aware of, such as an unconscious tendency to clench your hands into fists.

How to Breathe

Most of us breathe incorrectly much of the time. This is, we tend to breathe from the chest, rather than from the abdomen. When you are breathing correctly, from the abdomen, your belly *expands* as you breathe in, and *flattens* as you breathe out. The expansion of the abdomen indicates that the diaphragm is fully lowered, inflating the lungs to their fullest, and allowing a more efficient intake of oxygen.

"Belly breathing" is even more important during running than during your daily activities, because the act of running is designed to make you breathe hard and to exercise your entire oxygen-intake system. To get an idea of what belly breathing is like, sit straight in a chair and put your hand on your abdomen. Now, breathe in as deeply as possible, and as you do so, consciously push outward on your abdomen. You should be able to feel this expansion with your hand if you are doing it correctly. When you breathe out, suck in, trying to flatten your abdomen. Practice this a few times so you know how it feels, then try it when you are running.

One of the most painful things that can befall any runner is the dreaded "side stitch"—which you have probably experienced from time to time after exerting yourself in an unusual way, perhaps going for a long walk after a full meal, or running for a bus. This side stitch is actually a spasm of the diaphragm and is often caused by incorrect breathing. If you get a side stitch while running, sometimes it helps to exaggerate belly breathing: consciously force your abdomen out every time you breathe in; suck it in when you breathe out. It takes a moment or two to get the hang of this while you are actually running, but sometimes it can make the difference between stopping for the day and finishing a good run.

As to whether you should try to regulate your breathing while running, I can only advise you to do what feels natural. Some runners do put a lot of concentration into their breathing, breathing in, say, every third time the right foot strikes the ground, and breathing out over the space of two footfalls, or breathing in and out in response to some predetermined count. If you want to try such a system and it seems to work for you, fine, but it's not really necessary. If you let your body breathe naturally, as it wants to, you will find that your breathing is very regular. The few times I do pay attention to it, I usually notice that my breaths fall in a regular rhythm with my footsteps.

How Fast?

The fastest women runners can run a mile in well under five minutes, but in order to reach that goal they've had to train at a much slower pace over thousands of miles. For fitness-oriented runners, speed is the least important consideration. To find the best pace for you, simply run at a pace at which you can comfortably carry on a conversation. You can test this by finding someone to run with and actually talking to her, by humming or singing to yourself, or even by talking to yourself, if you don't mind raised eyebrows from bystanders. The idea of talking while running may seem unlikely, but it's easy and natural and won't interfere with your breathing in any way as long as you are running at the right pace. You may have heard the term "oxygen debt" used in connection with running—this situation occurs when your body is not delivering oxygen to your tissues as quickly as it is needed. As long as you run at a pace at which you can talk, you will never go into oxygen debt. If you do find yourself getting short of breath or breathing heavily at any point, simply slow down.

After you have been running for a while and have become more fit, you can work on stepping up your pace if you wish, but it's not necessary. The most comfortable pace for most beginning women runners is usually anywhere from eight to twelve minutes a mile—but if you are faster or slower, don't worry about it. Just keep on running.

Who Should and Shouldn't Run

Most women who are in average physical condition can probably start one of the programs described in this chapter—but just to be safe, see a doctor first. For best results, try to find a doctor who runs herself (or himself); if your present doctor doesn't run—and most don't—then call the physical director of your local Y or the local branch of Road Runners of America for the name of a doctor who does. This is important for three reasons: many of the benefits of running are only now being studied and may be unknown to a non-running doctor. In addition, there are some conditions which were formerly thought to be made worse by running (for example, varicose veins, which can be helped in many cases by running; see Chapter 6). A doctor who runs is likely to have the latest information on such conditions. And finally, above all, you want a doctor who knows from experience what a running program involves. If you have some physical condition that will cause you particular problems, it's vital that your doctor know exactly how running affects that condition, so that he or she can best advise you on going through with the program.

Your doctor may ask you to take a stress test before you begin your conditioning program. This test, which I mentioned in Chapter 2, allows the doctor to monitor your heart while you are under maximum physical stress. Stress-testing facilities are not yet available everywhere in the country, but their availability is rapidly growing.

Runner's World magazine recommends stress testing, if possible, to the following groups: those over thirty years old and beginning a running program for the first time; those starting, regardless of age, from an extremely bad condition—such as being obese, with extreme shortness of breath; those having a personal history of high blood pressure, rheumatic fever, diabetes, or other chronic severe illness; those with a family history of heart disease; and those suffering chronic chest pains, no matter what the suspected cause.

If your doctor discovers any abnormality in your heart, he or she will probably recommend that you stay longer on the walking part of the program, or may prescribe a more limited type of conditioning program.

Unfortunately, there are some people who should not take up an exercise program of any sort. Among them are those with severe heart disease, such as congenital valve disease, greatly enlarged heart, or *recent* heart attack; and those with high blood pressure that cannot be controlled by medication.

Other conditions also require caution. If you are very much overweight, for example, you should spend time on a walking program before you graduate to running; the good news here is that walking will help you get your weight down while you prepare to run. And of course you shouldn't undertake a vigorous exercise program if you have or are recovering from an infectious disease, such as flu or even a bad cold. If you are in doubt about any condition you may have that would affect your exercising—from flat feet to sneezing fits—ASK YOUR DOCTOR.

Warming Up

And now, at last, you're ready to begin running—well, almost ready. Before beginning any vigorous exercise, you should always spend a little time in warming up. How much time is up to you—it can be as little as five minutes, or as long as half an hour—but it's very important to do at least some warm-up work.

Why is the warm-up so important? Quite simply, because your

muscles and cardiovascular system should not be expected to start working suddenly at maximum efficiency without any warning. Muscles which have to start up from inactivity—or worse, from tension caused by your working at a desk all day—simply will not function at their top efficiency without a little time to loosen up. Even more important, a muscle not properly warmed up is subject to injury.

I learned the importance of warm-ups the hard way—through a recurring back problem. For the first six months or so of my running program I seldom warmed up, just went out to the track and started running. After several months I developed a spasm in my back that was occasionally so painful that I had to stop running for the day. My problem was finally diagnosed as a muscle strain caused in part by weak stomach muscles and by too-tight hamstrings (your hamstrings are the very important tendons that run down the backs of your thighs). The primary solution to the problem was to spend some time on loosening my hamstrings before I ran. The effect of doing these very simple hamstring warm-ups was spectacular—the problem lessened almost immediately. And the more time I spent on the warm-up, the less severe the back pain was. On those days when I was "in a hurry" and omitted my warm-ups (which generally take me all of about five minutes) the back pain would almost invariably return.

You probably don't have back pain or leg pain, and chances are you won't have when you begin running. But to make sure that you don't *get* any strains or pains, spend at least a minimal amount of time on warm-up exercises from the first day you start running. An ounce of prevention really is worth a pound of cure—especially when the ounce of prevention itself is simple and easy and feels very good.

The warm-up exercises described here are in two groups: minimum and supplemental. In addition, there is a note on other exercises. As you begin your running program, remember that the minimum warm-ups should *always* be done before running, and to them you may add one or more components from the supplemental group. All of these exercises are easy and will make your running more enjoyable.

Minimum warm-ups

1. Back stretcher. Bend over from the waist, keeping your legs straight, let your arms and head drop, and just *hang*. That's all. Don't try to bounce any closer to the ground, and don't tighten any of your muscles; just relax and let gravity do its work of unkinking your back and stretching the muscles and tendons of your back and legs. Hold for one minute. Repeat two or three times.

2. Heart warm-up. This warm-up should always constitute the first part of your run (or walk). It consists of either walking or jogging *very slowly* for the first few minutes to give your heart and lungs a chance to adjust to the increasing work load.

Supplemental warm-ups

Choose some or all of these on those days when you feel like having more of a warm-up. All are stretching exercises, and they should be performed with that idea in mind—don't bob or bounce, but consciously *stretch* the muscle groups involved. Bouncing can cause a muscle to do the opposite of what you want; that is, it will tend to tighten up rather than loosen. These exercises should follow the basic back stretcher.

1. Calf stretcher. Stand about two feet from a wall, facing it. Stretch out your arms and lean against the wall, supporting yourself with your hands. Keep your feet flat on the floor as you lean into the wall; then push yourself away from it, as if you were doing push-ups against it. You should feel a stretching in your back and hamstrings, but especially in your calf muscles. If you don't feel the stretch, move your feet farther away from the wall. Repeat very slowly three to five times.

2. Hamstring stretcher. Find a table or railing about waist high. Put one foot up on it, then bend down over your outstretched leg, reaching toward your toes with your hands. Hold on to any part of your leg, ankle, or foot that you can comfortably reach while still feeling a stretching in the back of your thigh. Your ultimate goal is to "lie down" along the leg, but don't go down any farther than is comfortable, and don't bounce. Hold the position without straining for thirty seconds, then repeat with the other leg. Repeat once with each leg.

3. Trunk circling. With your hands on your waist, and your back straight, bend forward slightly from the waist. Now slowly circle the top part of your body counterclockwise, feeling the stretching along your back and sides. Repeat two or three times, then reverse direction and repeat.

4. Slow sixteens. This exercise is an exception to the rule of no bouncing—but the bouncing you do should be *very* gentle, more of a prolonged stretch than a bounce. This is an especially good exercise to use for the last part of your warm-up, not only because it stretches several different muscle groups, but because it is vigorous enough to begin to warm up your heart and lungs. The exercise is in four parts, as follows:

First, stand with your legs comfortably apart. Now, bend over forward from the waist, only as far as is comfortable, and reach gently and slowly behind you with your outstretched arms between your legs. Maintaining this position, stretch to the back a total of sixteen times, then return to starting position.

Second, stretch your arms straight out at your sides and bend

a

b

c

forward from the waist, keeping your back straight and your trunk parallel to the ground. Again, stretch downward very gently sixteen times. Return to starting position.

Third, put your right hand on your waist, and stretch your left arm above your head. Now gently stretch to the right as far as you comfortably can, sixteen times. Return to starting position.

Fourth, reverse the position of the third step, putting your left hand on your waist and stretching your right arm above your head. Gently stretch to the left sixteen times. Return to starting position.

Now, repeat the entire sequence, only this time stretch *eight* times in each position. Repeat again, stretching *four* times, then *two*, and finally, *very* slowly, take one long stretch in each position. When you have finished this entire exercise, you should feel loose and relaxed all over and ready to begin your run.

Other exercises

You may have become interested in running in the first place because it is an exercise that will give you many benefits in a limited amount of time; the thought of doing anything beyond your basic warm-up and short run may seem wildly excessive at this point. I know how you feel—I had the same attitude when I started running, and I am still probably one of the ten laziest persons on my block.

But physical fitness, as you are about to discover, can become truly addictive; as you see yourself becoming firmer and feel yourself becoming healthier, you tend to want more and more. In a few months you may find yourself a fitness freak, ready to rush out and join a kung-fu class at the very least. If you do decide to step up your activity, you'll probably do very well because of your increased level of fitness. But in the meantime, as far as supplementary exercise is concerned, do only what you feel like doing.

There are literally hundreds of different exercises that you can choose from—from standard calisthenics to complicated and im-possible-looking yoga asanas. You probably already know how to do many of these exercises, and if you don't it is easy enough to find out, through various books or by joining a local gym, Y, or exercise class.

The only supplemental exercise that I urge you to make time for at this point is sit-ups. Why sit-ups? Because a great many American women, and you may be among them, tend to have weak abdominal muscles. And weak abdominal muscles are a major cause of back pain—if your abdomen can't quite do its job of holding everything in place, excessive strain is placed on your back. It's true that running will tone and strengthen the muscles all over your body, but it will also tend to strengthen your back muscles more, *relatively*, than your abdominal muscles. If you have somewhat weak abdominal muscles to begin with, the imbalance between the two sets of muscles after you've run for a few months might cause you some problems.

To guard against developing back pain—and to ensure a smooth, flat belly—it makes sense to spend a little time strengthening those abdominal muscles. The very best exercise for this purpose is sit-ups—done properly. Here is the recommended way to do sit-ups in order to strengthen your abdomen:

Lie on your back with your hands clasped behind your head and your knees bent. (Yes, *bent!* Straight-legged sit-ups not only put abnormal stress on your knees and back but do little to firm your stomach muscles.) Try to anchor your feet under a heavy piece of furniture, or get someone to hold your ankles down for you. The purpose of this is to assure that the exercise will be performed smoothly and without any jerking. If you can't find some way to anchor your feet, then just try to do the exercise as smoothly as possible. Now come up slowly, rolling vertebra-by-vertebra off the floor. Touch your bent elbows to your knees. Roll back down, still slowly and smoothly, feeling your back unwind bone by bone. Rest a few seconds and repeat. Work up to twenty-five or thirty repetitions, but work up slowly, perhaps adding only two or three repetitions per week. The important thing is to do the sit-ups without strain and with as little jerking as possible.

If you find it too hard to do even one complete sit-up, then start with half-sit-ups. You do these in the same basic position, but with your arms at your sides. Raise only your head, chest, shoulders, and arms, then roll back down. After you have done repetitions of half-sit-ups for a few weeks, you should find it easier to proceed with full sit-ups.

Some women find it painful to do any kind of sit-ups on a hard floor; if you have this problem, try to do your sit-ups on a thick rug, a folded towel or a blanket.

Warming Down

"Cooling off," "warming down"—these seemingly contradictory phrases apply to the final process in your running program: giving your body a chance to slow back down to normal after vigorous exercise.

There are no special exercises you need to do while warming down—but NEVER stop running abruptly. Always walk around for at least five minutes after you have finished running. You can continue to walk around the track you have been running on—or just walk slowly home. The important thing is to resist the temptation to sit down or lie down—or you could pass out from a shortage of blood to your brain.

How do you know when you have cooled off enough? After a while, you'll be able to tell from the way your body feels. But while you're still a beginner, it's a good idea to count your pulse five minutes after you have begun warming down. To do this, stop walking temporarily and find a pulse—the easiest place is in your throat, on either side of your Adam's apple. Using a watch with a second hand, count your pulse for ten seconds, then multiply the result by six. This will give you your heart rate per minute. If that number is over 120 after five minutes of warming down, then you have exercised too vigorously and should go slower next time. You should also keep walking until your pulse rate is below 120.

As you walk to warm down you may enjoy doing other loosening-up exercises—such as rolling your shoulders from front to back, or arm circling.

This walking warm-down completes your daily running routine, but if you want to loosen up further, and to help prevent sore muscles—especially if you are just beginning or have run more than usual—the following two yoga exercises are especially good.

1. Half-forward bend. Sit on the floor, with your legs stretched out in front of you. With your right leg straight, and keeping both legs on the floor, bend your left leg and bring your left foot as close to your body as possible (ideally, it should rest just at your crotch). Now, without bending your right knee, reach forward with both hands and grasp your right leg, ankle, or foot, as far down as you can reach without straining. Ideally, your body should rest along the length of the leg, your head on your knee and your fingers grasping your toes, but don't push for this extreme position—go only as far as is comfortable. Hold for thirty seconds, relaxing consciously. Reverse the position and repeat with your other leg. This exercise will help loosen up tight leg muscles and is also good for stretching your back; in addition it is a good supplemental hamstring stretcher.

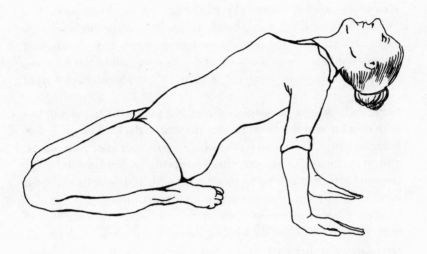

2. Foot exercise. This position can be a little painful at first, so go slow until you get used to it.

First, sit on your heels, with your toes bent against the floor, and

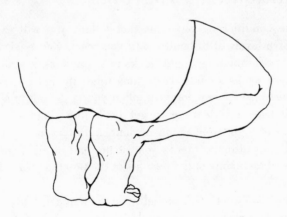

your knees together in front of you. Put your hands to your side, then "walk" them back as far as is comfortable. Now, drop your head back and arch your body upward. Your weight is on your toes, hands, and knees. Hold for five to thirty seconds. To come out of the position, relax your body, raise your head, and "walk" your hands back to your sides.

Second, change the position of your foot so that the top of your foot is in contact with the floor. Repeat the rest of the exercise as before (your weight will now rest on the whole top of your foot, your hands, and your knees). This exercise is especially good for relieving tension in the feet and for improving strength and flexibility. It feels best when you have been running longer than usual.

Many other yoga asanas, indeed any relaxing, stretching type of exercise, are also good for winding down after a workout. After you have been running for a while, you will have a better idea of what feels right for you.

Conditioning Programs

In the conditioning programs that follow, you will exercise at progressive levels of difficulty until you reach your goal. This will take from a minimum of eight weeks to as much as several months. Even eight weeks sounds like a long time, though it's not, really, when you consider how long it's taken you to get out of shape. It's going to take a little time to get back into shape—maybe the minimum of eight weeks, maybe longer. But even if you haven't reached your ultimate fitness goal at the end of eight weeks, you should still feel many of the benefits of the program well within that time.

The first two weeks will probably be the hardest. Although you'll undoubtedly have a psychological high because you're doing something good for yourself, physically you will often feel tired and sore, and even discouraged at times. But then, after three to eight weeks, something else will happen. You'll begin to feel so energetic and full of life you'll wonder why you didn't start running years ago. If you bear in mind that these early weeks won't be altogether pleasant, it may be easier to commit yourself to the program for at least eight weeks. If at the end of that time you've decided that running isn't for you—well, nobody can say you didn't give it a fair chance.

The conditioning program you choose will require a little more time than the program you'll follow to maintain yourself in good condition. This is because a conditioning program should be followed four times a week for best results; once you're in shape, you can maintain fitness with just three workouts a week (although four is better). In fact, your minimum maintenance program will involve only sixty minutes of actual running per week, which is only one hour out of 168—not much time to put in for a healthy, fit body.

I have provided a choice of two running conditioning programs— one based on how far you run, the other on the amount of time run. Whichever you choose, remember to *start slowly*. Don't rush. Don't try to get ahead of the program. You can vary the time and days that you run, but don't try to run farther or sooner than suggested. If you do, one of two things might happen: you might injure yourself, or you might exhaust yourself to the point where you give up running forever. A little patience for only a few weeks is all you need to set yourself firmly on the road to lifelong fitness.

Both running conditioning programs begin with at least one week of walking. Why walking? Because your body will need time to adjust to the new activity you are about to ask it to perform. Not only are your heart and lungs unaccustomed to vigorous exercise, but your feet, ankles, and legs—and all their muscles, tendons, and joints—need to get used to supporting you for a sustained period of time.

While you remain in the walking part of a conditioning program, you needn't wear track clothes—although you may prefer to. You *should* wear your running shoes and socks, though. You can walk anywhere—but if you're planning to walk around the neighborhood rather than on a track, remember that your activity must be continuous for aerobic benefit, so try to avoid busy intersections where you'll have to wait for the light to change.

How long should you stay in the walking program? Well, that depends a great deal on your age and physical condition. *Everyone* should begin with at least one week of walking only (Level I). After that, add one more week of walking for each five years of age over twenty-five, as summarized in Table 1. However, if you're in better-than-average condition, or if you do a great deal of walking as a matter of course, you may not need to spend several weeks walking. The principal thing to keep in mind is *not* to progress to the next level until you can comfortably walk thirty minutes, four times a week. By "comfortably" I mean without getting tired or out of breath.

Table 1.   Suggested Weeks at Level I (Walking Only)

AGE	WEEKS
up to 25	1
26–30	2
31–35	3
36–40	4
41–45	5
46–50	6
51–55	7
56–60	8
over 60	You should spend at least 9–10 weeks in a walking program, and may find you feel so well you never need to progress beyond this level. If you do want to go on, check with your doctor

Note: Women of all ages should spend more time at Level I if they are overweight. A good rule of thumb is to add one week of walking for every five pounds overweight. (See Chapter 9, page 143.)

The same holds true for every other Level of the program. If you are over twenty-five or out of shape, or both, you may have to add extra weeks as needed. Again, never progress beyond any Level until you can perform it *comfortably* the required number of times.

Even those women under twenty-five will probably not proceed in a straight line from Level I to Level VIII in only eight weeks, though they will probably progress more rapidly at some stages than at others. The Levels in these programs are only guidelines—if you are doing too much, your body will tell you so! If at some point you must stop for a while—say you get sick or go on vacation—then drop back to a lower Level. Take about as much time as you missed to get back in condition. If any Level seems too difficult, then drop back to the previous Level. Spend as much time at any Level as you need. Remember, you're not in a race! And every step you take, walking or running, brings you that much closer to your goal of fitness and health.

Distance program and time program

The exercise at each Level of either program must be performed four times a week to be effective. For best results, try to space the days out: two or even three days in a row is okay, but try not to do all your week's exercise in four consecutive days. Many women find it easiest to schedule three workouts during the week and one on the weekend, but how you structure your four days depends on you and your own busy schedule.

The two programs—one based on the distance run, the other on the amount of time spent running—are designed to provide about the same amount of exercise at the same Levels. If you are running on one program and get bored, you could switch to the other without hurting your progress.

The eight Levels of each program are summarized in the table below. Both programs begin with one week (minimum) of walking; the amount of running is then gradually increased from a minimum at Level II up to Level VIII, when you will run continuously. When you are able comfortably to complete the goal of either time or distance for any Level, then you are ready to move on to the next.

Table 2.   Walking–Running Conditioning Programs

	DISTANCE PROGRAM	TIME PROGRAM	
LEVEL	GOAL		FREQUENCY
I Walk	30 min	30 min	4 × wk
II Walk-run	1½ mi (2½ km)	30 min	4 × wk
III Walk-run	1½ mi (2½ km)	30 min	4 × wk
IV Walk-run	1½ mi (2½ km)	25 min	4 × wk
V Run-walk	1½ mi (2½ km)	20-25 min	4 × wk
VI Run-walk	1½ mi (2½ km)	20 min	4 × wk
VII Run-walk	1½ mi (2½ km)	15-20 min	4 × wk
VIII Run	1½ mi (2½ km)	15 min	4 × wk

What to do at each Level (for both programs)

LEVEL I: WALKING.

Walk continuously, wherever you wish, at any pace that is comfortable for you. If you find thirty minutes of walking too exhausting, or if your feet begin to bother you, then start with twenty or even fewer minutes of walking your first week(s). Do not move beyond Level I until you can *comfortably* walk thirty minutes, four times a week.

LEVEL II: WALKING AND RUNNING.

Now you are ready to add a little running to your program. But only a little. Walk for a while, as in Level I, then start to run very slowly, just until you start to feel winded; then walk again. When you are no longer huffing and puffing, but before you are completely cooled down, try a little more running. If this seems too strenuous, then just continue walking at a comfortable pace. The idea is to exert yourself *continuously,* but never to the point of breathlessness or real fatigue.

LEVEL III: WALKING AND RUNNING.

Add more running than in Level II—run at least twice during the period, more if you feel like it, but *don't strain.*

LEVEL IV: WALKING AND RUNNING.

Add more running. You should now be running about a third of the time: say, half a mile (though probably not continuously) in the distance program, eight minutes or so in the time program.

LEVEL V: RUNNING AND WALKING.

You should now be running and walking about equal amounts.

LEVEL VI: RUNNING AND WALKING.

Continue to add running, without straining. Your goal at this Level should be to run a total of about a mile, or a total of about ten to twelve minutes.

LEVEL VII: RUNNING AND WALKING.

You are now running during most of the workout, walking only as needed to catch your breath.

LEVEL VIII: RUNNING.

Congratulations. You are a runner. You are now running a mile and a half or fifteen to twenty minutes without stopping.

Table 3.   Maintenance Programs

DISTANCE PROGRAM	TIME PROGRAM	
GOAL		FREQUENCY
1½ mi (2½ km)	15 min	4 × wk
2 mi (3.2 km)	20 min	3 × wk

Maintenance

The "maintenance level" is the program you should follow to maintain your new-found fitness. The distances and times suggested are the minimum amount of running you will need to do to stay in shape.

Of course you can do more if you like, and you will find that if you do decide to add more running, the good effects of aerobics training will increase. I have found that I feel best psychologically and physically when I run about ten to twelve miles a week (usually in four or five workouts), though I feel all right and don't seem to lose any of the benefits when I run less.

If you decide to step up your maintenance program, it's far better to increase your distance or the amount of time run than to try to improve your speed. Researchers are finding that long, slow, distance running is better for building a base of endurance and health than any kind of faster work, such as sprinting. Furthermore, the energy expenditure (calories burned) is approximately the same per mile no matter what your speed. (I know this sounds incredible, but it's true. You burn around 100 calories for your ten-minute mile, while the speedster who keeps passing you also burns about 100 calories for his six-minute mile. Of course if he runs the same amount of *time* as you, he'll burn more calories because he'll run more miles.)

If you decide to increase the number of workouts per week, that's all right too, but for best results any one workout should involve at least twelve to fifteen minutes of running. There are many runners who run every single day; others who feel worn out if they run more than every other day. After you have been running for a few months, you will naturally settle into the routine of times per week and distance or time per run that is right for your body.

Bear in mind that if for some reason you have to stop working out altogether, most of your aerobics benefits will be lost in only five weeks—so you'll have to start out very slowly when you resume.

It is a good idea to keep some sort of record of your running, not just to keep track of the program you're on, but because seeing the totals in black and white can act as a real incentive to keep you going. A running log can also help you find your own best running pattern, by giving you a general idea of the amount you have run over a given period, the days on which you tend to slack off, and the spacing of your workouts. Most important, a running log lets you see the progress you have made, which is especially valuable in the first few weeks of your program. On the next page is a chart to get you started, with a couple of sample weeks filled in. When you have completed either program, continue to record your distance or time run, at least until you have settled into a comfortable maintenance routine.

Your Heart Rate

Earlier, I advised running at a pace at which you can comfortably carry on a conversation. Nearly all experts agree that this indicates the ideal pace for training; of course this pace can vary from a twelve-minute mile for beginners to a six-minute mile for marathoners.

There is another way to determine the best pace for you, and that is to base it on your heart rate.

Four aspects of the heart rate are important to runners. These are the resting rate, or your pulse rate when you aren't doing anything;

Running Log

Sun	Mon	Tues	Wed	Thu	Fri	Sat	Level	Comments
30 min.	1½ mi.	1½ mi.		1½ mi.		1½ mi.	mount.	Good week!
		30 min.		30 min.		30 min.	I a	not as hard as I thought but my feet hurt!

the maximum rate, which is the fastest your heart can beat without collapse; the training rate, or the rate your heart beats during exercise; and the recovery rate, which is a measure of how quickly your heart returns to normal after running.

The recovery rate is considered by some experts to be the most important indicator of a healthy cardiovascular system; you are monitoring this rate when you check to see whether your pulse has gone below 120 five minutes after exercise. By monitoring another heart rate, the training rate, you can check to see if you are training at the right pace for you.

There are many complex formulas for determining your ideal pulse rate during exercise; as a matter of fact, there is some disagreement among doctors over what the ideal rate is. But to get an approximate idea of the *maximum* training rate for you, simply subtract your age from 170. For example, if you are thirty-two, then the *maximum* rate your heart should beat during exercise is 138 beats a minute. To see if you are exercising within your maximum, stop running and immediately count your pulse for six seconds. Add a zero to the total, and you will have an approximation of your heart rate per minute during exercise. (When you finish taking your pulse, either resume running or begin warming down.) If your pulse is faster than the maximum for your age, then you should slow down until you have become more fit.

Running in Place

On occasion, running in place can be substituted for running, but most women find it boring and uncomfortable, and few ever stick with it as a regular exercise program. Still, running in place is better than not running at all, and you might want to start with it if you're shy about exercising in public.

Because it's not practical to mix walking with running in place (although a walking program would be an excellent supplement), you simply build up the amount of time you spend running in place, progressively, over several weeks. Your goal is to run in place for fifteen minutes, four times a week, at a comfortable heart training rate (roughly, around 120–140 beats per minute—but be careful not to exceed your maximum training rate). Following is a program for running in place; as with the running programs, you should remain at each Level until you can perform it comfortably.

LEVEL I: one minute, slowly
LEVEL II: 1–2 minutes, a little faster
LEVEL III: 2–4 minutes
LEVEL IV: 4–6 minutes
LEVEL V: 6–8 minutes
LEVEL VI: 8–10 minutes
LEVEL VII: 10–12 minutes
LEVEL VIII: 12–15 minutes
Maintenance Level: 15 minutes, four times a week

Women who run in place often develop foot and ankle problems. To help avoid such injuries, always wear good running shoes with at least one pair of socks, and run on the softest surface you can find: a special "jogging pad" or very thick carpet is best. Just as with running on a track, it is important to warm up before running in place, and then to warm down by walking around the room for a while.

It's obvious that I don't really like running in place; but to be fair, I should point out that some women are very successful with such a program, at least for a few months. Most of those I know watch TV while they exercise, or play records or listen to the news. I have one friend who ran in place for months before she began running outside. Her special trick was to tape-record songs with a beat at the pace she wanted to run, then combine them so the tape lasted exactly as long as she exercised.

One possible problem for women who live in apartments is that their downstairs neighbors may (justifiably) try to have them evicted. If you can't schedule your running in place for a time when there's nobody home downstairs, try running out in the hall or even down in the basement—on a stack of old carpeting remnants.

Finally, if you run in place for several weeks and then decide to move to a regular running program, you will probably have to start at a very low Level; even though your heart and lungs may be conditioned, your feet and legs won't be, as somewhat different muscular movements are involved.

What to Expect

Now you are really a runner. So what if you can run only a few yards at first? The important thing is that you have embarked on a lifelong program that will keep you feeling and looking great no matter what your age. You have every right to feel good about yourself.

The next few weeks won't be the easiest in your life—but I can guarantee that things will only get easier and pleasanter as you run longer and longer. To help you keep your feet moving toward your goal, here are some hints on what to expect in the first weeks of your running program.

First, the bad news. I can practically promise that at times you'll feel like chucking the whole thing and want to go back to being an unfit slob. You'll be bored and unhappy. You'll be irritable. You'll wish you'd never heard of running. And there's a reason for these feelings: in the first few weeks of a running program, although your body is becoming fitter, you aren't experiencing most of the beneficial changes yet. What you are experiencing, mainly, is fatigue—as tired, out-of-condition muscles, including your heart and lungs, begin to take on new and unaccustomed tasks.

Don't let these feelings get you down. All beginning runners experience them. Just remember the commitment you made before you began the program—that you would stick it out for eight weeks. That's only thirty-two times of going out and exercising, and thirty-two times of anything isn't really very much.

But things will get better. And they won't get better gradually: they'll get better in sudden, dramatic spurts of improvement. For days you may be stuck at one Level—you just can't get the energy to run more than a sixteenth of a mile, and you don't think it will ever change—and then suddenly, with no warning, one day you go out and find you can run with ease three times that distance. Doctors don't know just how or why this "plateau effect" works, but thousands of runners and other athletes can attest to it.

Instead of being bored and depressed, you may have the opposite reaction. You may feel so high on yourself, so good about actually doing something for yourself, that you start to overdo it. You may train six days a week instead of four, or try to run farther than your muscles and cardiovascular system are ready for. That is just as big a mistake as getting discouraged and giving up, and for two reasons. The first is that it can be dangerous to your health to undertake more exercise than you are ready for. If you ask untrained muscles to suddenly take on an unaccustomed task, they can become injured, and you may find yourself unable to run at all. Or your muscles may become so sore that you swing to the opposite pole, and get discouraged and depressed—and quit.

My friend Susan illustrates the dangers of too much enthusiasm. When she began a running program she plunged into it with the verve she brings to most endeavors. One morning she called me after her run to tell me how excited and great she felt now that she was running. I congratulated her on sticking with her program, we chatted awhile, and then, just before she hung up, she asked me tentatively:

"Just one more thing. What do you do about the pain?"

"What pain?"

"In your legs. I mean, it's okay during the day—I hardly notice it—but at night when I lie down I can't get out of bed. Last night I had to ask my husband to bring me a glass of water because I couldn't walk."

"Wait a minute," I said. "How far are you running?"

"Well, I'm up to half a mile now, and I was thinking of trying for three-quarters next week."

Susan had been running for only two weeks, after years of inactivity! I almost laughed, but her problem was too serious. I advised her to cut way down on the running she was doing and to mix it with more walking. She followed my advice, and the pains in her legs promptly disappeared.

Moral: If, after beginning a running program, your legs are so sore that you can't walk—then you're overdoing it!

There are other signs that you're overdoing. If you notice any of the following symptoms during or after exercise, you're probably moving too fast; you should remain longer on the Level you are on, or even drop back to a lower Level. These signs are rapid heartbeat and breathlessness five to ten minutes after you have stopped exercising; nausea or vomiting during or after exercise (this is most common if you are running too *fast*); extreme fatigue lasting up to twenty-four hours after exercise; insomnia; or excessive need for sleep.

Even if you don't overdo your workouts, you will probably experience some random aches and pains—nothing so bad, say, as going to the dentist, but enough to cause some discomfort. You probably won't experience all these reactions, but expect some of them. First of all, your legs will probably hurt—not excruciatingly, but enough to let you know you have been working out. This pain may be anywhere but is most common in the calf muscles. Your ankles, too, may become sore, and sometimes slightly swollen. This is nothing to worry about and will go away with time. Your buttocks may become sore—a sign that your derrière is starting to tighten up. Your breasts may hurt because your pectoral muscles are getting a workout from the arm action of running. If you find this a real problem, try wearing a tighter bra.

Other body changes you may notice include loss of weight, or at least of inches—a loss that will be visible in a very few weeks. You will probably find you want to drink more fluids, to replace the water lost during perspiration, and your appetite may change. If you run just before a meal, you may find that you have very little appetite; on the other hand, some women find that their appetites increase to make up for the calorie expenditure of running. If your goal is to lose weight, then you'll have to resist the temptation to appease your increased appetite.

As you continue to run, you'll find that you have some bad days when you don't seem to have any energy at all. Don't worry about it—even women who routinely run ten or more miles a day experience times when everything is blah and the workout isn't much fun. But those bad days are balanced by equally good days, when everything seems to come together and you feel as if you're flying over the course, your mind and body in complete harmony, your soul at peace with the world. It's those days that make it all worthwhile, the days when you know you are a complete human being who affirms with every step: "I am a runner!"

5

For Women Only

"**E**ACH of us is an experiment of one."—*Dr. George Sheehan.*

Dr. Sheehan, a physician, runner and writer, is speaking here of the chance for each of us to achieve her potential in body, soul and mind. The experiment comes in discovering your own limits and learning what balance of activity, challenge and contemplation will achieve that potential for you.

To women athletes, Dr. Sheehan's statement applies in another way, which Dr. Sheehan probably did not intend. For each time a woman takes up a sport formerly considered closed to our sex, she is moving into unknown territory. How does athletic activity affect menstruation, pregnancy, menopause? How does each of these things in turn affect athletic activity? The answers to these questions are by no means certain, because the questions themselves have only just begun to be asked. A very few studies have been done in some areas of sports medicine that apply to women only; but for the most part, each of us must rely on common sense, the advice of doctors, and the experience of other women runners. In this chapter we will look at some of these aspects of running that affect women only.

Premenstrual Problems

Some fortunate women go through their entire lives without ever having the least discomfort stemming from their menstrual periods: no premenstrual tension, no cramps, no bloating, no heavy flow. Others have one or more of these symptoms more or less often. Still other women find the whole experience a nightmare and try not to think about it between times.

Wherever you fit in the above categories, once you are a runner you may wonder about running and your period. Is it safe to run during your period? Is it beneficial? Will running be easier? Harder? Unfortunately there are no definitive answers to these questions: too few studies have been made. The best advice I can give you is to become your own experiment of one and find out what is right for your own body. In the meantime, based on the few studies that have been made, the following answers seem to be true for many women.

The most common problem associated with the menstrual cycle is the collection of symptoms known as premenstrual syndrome. While these symptoms vary from woman to woman, and even from month to month in the same woman, most women seem to experience some of them at least sometimes in their lives. These symptoms include headache, irritability, depression, shakiness, temporary weight gain, and swelling in the ankles, breasts and abdomen.

Not surprisingly, such premenstrual symptoms are the ones reported most often by women runners as giving problems in relation to running. Many women say that they feel more tired and less energetic on the days just before their periods. "I'm tense," one woman says. "I don't seem to have any energy, and my legs get tired much faster." Other women express similar feelings: "My speed and times always go down," says my friend Kathy. "And sometimes my breasts get so sore I can't run at all."

Painful breasts are a common problem of women runners during the premenstrual days; most of the tenderness is probably caused by water retention. Some women tend to retain so much water that their weight can temporarily increase by as much as five pounds or more—no wonder they find their times and speed going down! If you are one of the many women who sometimes have these problems, you will probably just have to face the fact that there will be some days during the month when you won't feel like going out and running and when you shouldn't try to push for better speed or time. If your major problem is water retention, ask your gynecologist to prescribe a diuretic. As far as other symptoms go, though, you'll just have to grin and bear it: your monthly cycle will have an effect on your running.

But what about the other way around? Does running affect your premenstrual problems? Well, again, not all the evidence is in (in fact, the scientists aren't even looking for any in most cases), but the answer seems to be *yes:* running does affect premenstrual problems—and it affects them in a positive way. In one of the few studies so far made, Finnish researchers discovered that athletic participation of any sort seems to alleviate the symptoms of premenstrual syndrome. And according to a survey of nearly one hundred women runners, reported on by Janet Heinonen in *Runner's World* magazine, most women long-distance runners have found the same thing. The women I have spoken to agree for the most part. My friend Kathy, who retains a lot of water before her period, usually tries to run during this time anyway. "Even though I feel dragged out, running seems to help," she reports. "It definitely relieves tension." Another friend, Susan, is even more enthusiastic. "As far as I'm concerned," she says, "nothing beats it. Fifteen minutes of running is equivalent to a Darvon or four or five aspirins."

What about you? Well, you're the only one who knows how you feel, but I'd advise you at least to try to run on those premenstrual days. Even if you drag around the track or limp through the park for half your normal distance, you'll probably be glad you made the effort, because there's a good chance you'll feel a lot better when you've finished.

Menstruation

In some primitive societies, menstruating women are locked up in a special house, away from the men, so they won't contaminate anything. In others, women are considered to have special powers (usually evil) during their periods, and again are kept away from other people until they are "normal" again. In our advanced, civilized society, many women are taught from the time they are little girls that something is "wrong" with them during their periods, that they are sick and weak—and, at least partly as a result of this treatment, many of us do feel sick and weak during menstruation.

Although the entire approach to physical education for girls is changing, in many gym classes in the U.S. girls are still excused from gym on the days they are having their periods. Many of us have been taught that we are in a weakened condition at this time, and so we are used to doing as little as possible while we are menstruating, if not actually taking to bed. Because of these years of conditioning, the thought of any really strenuous activity seems foreign and a little dangerous to most of us—almost against the laws of nature.

Unfortunately, what most of us *didn't* know all these years was that doing something strenuous might have been just what we needed to help avoid menstrual problems in the first place. Running not only seems to relieve cramps in many women but also helps to *prevent* them in some cases. If you're one of the many women who (whether for psychological or physiological reasons or both) sometimes get cramps, low backache, or diarrhea on the first day or two of their period, try running on the day you start. The majority of women runners who get cramps report that the act of running stops or lessens the discomfort. As for me, although most of my menstrual problems have diminished in general since I've been running, until recently I didn't run at all when I had cramps; I was afraid the activity would somehow make the pain worse. Finally one day I ran anyway—and to my amazement the cramps disappeared almost as soon as I started to run. They returned a few hours later, but were much less severe, and on many occasions they have disappeared altogether after I ran.

Since doctors don't know exactly why some women have cramps, they don't know why running helps. According to one woman doctor, the increased blood flow may help to ease congestion in the pelvic area. In addition, running helps relieve tension, and tension can be a major contributor to the discomfort of cramps.

Whether or not you have cramps or other menstrual discomfort, you may find that as on those premenstrual days, you feel somewhat less energetic during your period. However, Olympic records have been set by athletes during their periods, and many women runners find that once their period actually starts, they feel more energetic than at other times during the month. Once again, it's a question of finding what's right for you. But unless you have extremely severe or unusual problems, don't use your period as an excuse not to run. Not only will you be missing a day's workout, but you may be avoiding the one thing that can ease the discomfort that's keeping you inside.

Contraceptives

Another of the many things that men runners don't ever have to consider is the effect of birth control on their athletic performance. (Naturally, you don't have to worry about this either unless you are on the Pill or have an I.U.D.) Since so few studies have been done of women runners in any context, not surprisingly there is very little information available on how contraceptives affect running and vice versa. I do know one woman marathoner who reported that she could hardly run at all while she was taking the Pill: "I was bloated all the time and just didn't have any energy. I almost quit running, but I gave up the Pill instead." Another woman marathoner, though, has a very real problem with the I.U.D.: "I can't run a very long race during my period," she reports. "Since I got the I.U.D. my period's so heavy I soak through anything in about an hour." Unless you are planning to run very long distances, this shouldn't be a problem for you, though some women report that their flow seems to increase temporarily after they run, whether or not they wear an I.U.D.

Pregnancy

What about running during pregnancy?

Here, even more than at other times, you should check with your doctor before you even consider running. Once again, you will probably get the best advice if you go to a doctor who herself runs, or who is sympathetic to running and other sports.

Until very recently, the view of modern medicine has been that women should take it as easy as possible while they are pregnant; certainly this is still true for women with certain conditions (such as a history of previous miscarriages). But when humankind was evolving in prehistoric times, there was no time or place to take it easy, no weekly or monthly obstetrical checkups; the daily work of gathering food and taking care of the cave had to continue whether the woman was pregnant or not. Furthermore, it is routine today in many cultures for a woman to remain active, often working out in the fields, right up until the day of delivery.

Most exercise-oriented doctors today would probably agree with Dr. Evelyn Gendel, director of the Kansas Division of Maternal and Child Health, that there's no reason not to continue to run *if you're continuing what's normal for you.* In other words, pregnancy is probably not the time to *start* a vigorous exercise program, but if you have been running all along and want to continue, and if your pregnancy is normally implanted, then by all means do continue. Exercise will help you maintain good muscle tone and may help to prevent back problems.

How much running should you do while you're expecting? Again, this question is best answered by your own doctor. Almost certainly she'll advise you not to try any marathons—and possibly nothing more than a slow jog at half your usual distance. Beyond that, and within her guidelines, listen to your body and do what feels right. Most women runners who have continued to run during pregnancy find that they tire more easily and can't maintain their usual distance and speed—but they also find that they seem to need the emotional and physical release of running more than at other times.

How far into the pregnancy should you continue to run? Again, this question will have different answers depending on your body and what your doctor tells you. Many doctors advise their patients to quit running at six months, particularly if there is some previous problem, such as a history of miscarriages. Other doctors allow their patients to continue to run as long as they like.

Some women runners have continued to run at least minimal distances through the ninth month. Trina Hosmer, who was on the 1972 American Olympic cross-country ski team, ran four miles two hours before her first child was born!

"I'd been feeling sort of strange all day," she reports, "but we'd miscalculated the time, so it never occurred to me I was in labor. I decided to go out and run, since it usually makes me feel better physically. I started getting cramps while I was running, and as soon as I stopped they became very intense. I barely had time to get home and change. I arrived at the hospital at 4:00 P.M., and my son was born at 4:52."

Hosmer has a close friend who also ran up till the last week of pregnancy, and who also had a very short labor. "Running definitely seems to speed up labor," Hosmer says. "Maybe more women ought to know about it."

Trina Hosmer's case is unusual in more ways than one. She was lucky to have an extremely understanding doctor throughout her pregnancy. "He told me that my main problem would probably be car wrecks caused by drivers gaping at the crazy pregnant lady in her track shoes."

Most women who run while pregnant take no special precautions and don't wear any special clothing or support; most also report that though they tire more quickly while running, the exercise does seem to ease their backaches.

Obviously Trina Hosmer and women like her are exceptional, but if you want to run during your pregnancy and if your doctor agrees, you can feel safe running for as long as it's comfortable. If you prefer to stop, though, or if your doctor advises you to stop, then—with your doctor's permission—you should try to walk as much as possible, up to an hour a day, to help maintain your muscle tone and aerobic conditioning.

If you do run you may find, as many women athletes have, that your labor is short and your delivery relatively easy and relaxed.

As for how soon you can begin to run after childbirth, again, it's best to consult your doctor. Most women runners don't resume exercise for at least a month to six weeks, though some start as soon as two weeks after delivery.

Motherhood

Nina Kuscsik didn't start running competitively until her thirties, when she had already borne three children. Today, she is one of the top distance runners in the country: in 1972 she was the first winner of the women's division of the Boston Marathon. Miki Gorman, who was forty at the time, came in second in the New York Marathon in 1975, only eight months after giving birth to her first baby. Hundreds of other women all over the world have successfully taken up running for the first time after they had children, or returned to it after time out for childbearing. In short, there is no more reason (other than lack of time) for a woman not to run after becoming a mother than for a man to stop running after becoming a father.

However, running *after* you have had children can sometimes present more problems than running while you are pregnant, for the simple reason that a new mother suddenly finds herself with far less time and energy than she used to have. Since more demands are being made on her limited energy, this is a time in which the benefits of running are more necessary than ever, but it is common for women runners to stop running altogether, or to cut back considerably on their time or mileage as soon as they become mothers.

"It was a nightmare," one young mother says of her baby's first year. "I was in school full time, and I had a child, and something simply had to go. I felt physically lousy most of the time, but there didn't really seem to be a choice."

Now that her child is older, this woman is running again, but she says that if she had it to do over, she would have tried harder to find some way to maintain her running program in that first year. By sharing the responsibility with their husbands, especially if the husbands themselves are runners, many women runners can solve the problem of handling a young baby and continuing to run. "We take turns watching the baby and running," reports a young Massachusetts woman. "We kind of miss running together, but it's worth it—and we're really looking forward to the time when Debbie's old enough to run with us."

Other running mothers get together, one watching the children while the other runs. A very few Y's and gyms have babysitting facilities during limited hours. If you can't find another solution, perhaps you and other mothers in your area could get together and petition your local Y to begin such a program for a few hours every week.

Judy Pollock, an Olympic racer from Australia, combined running with motherhood in a unique way. According to *Runner's World,* Pollock once marked out a strip of road in front of her house to practice running, darting into the house from time to time to check on dinner and make sure the children were still asleep.

Family Running

However you solve the logistics of combining running and motherhood, most married runners find that running is more pleasant and motivation easier if the whole family is involved. Countless numbers of women runners began running because their husbands ran. The reverse has been true in a few situations as well: as a man sees his wife become slimmer and healthier and younger looking, he decides that there may be something to running after all, and joins her on the track or roads.

The whole family, of course, includes children. This may seem to rule out running as a family sport, but here's the big surprise: children are natural distance runners! If you've ever spent an afternoon with children under ten, you know that for fairly long periods of time they seem to have an inexhaustible supply of energy. That energy can be well turned to running. According to Dr. Ernst van Aaken, women and children are better suited for long-distance running than men are, their hearts being larger in proportion to body size. And a recent study in the Soviet Union indicated that distance running at a moderate pace seems to be good for children—certainly far better for them than trying to sprint short distances at full speed. Young bodies may not be able to take the stresses of intense competition at short distances (those distances often offered in school track events), but children of all ages seem to enjoy and thrive on running longer distances.

The moral of this is that there's no reason not to take your children with you when you run. If you run at a slow enough pace, they can probably keep up with you. If you're running on a track and they get bored, they can always sit on the sidelines or play in the grass. I know that at my local track every month I see more and more families with their children, and often the children are out there running alongside Mommy or Daddy or both. (Too often, however, they are running in sandals or street shoes; if you decide to initiate your children into the joys of running, be sure to buy them good running shoes.) Running with your children can not only help to bring your family closer together, it can also help to break down some of the artificial barriers between the generations: for an hour or two a few times a week, at least, the kids get a chance to take part in an adult activity, while the adults can act like kids.

The final argument in favor of family running is perhaps the most obvious: the poor physical condition of most Americans is not limited to adults. Every month a new and alarming report comes out describing the poor health and fitness levels of American children. The possible causes for this sad situation range from a diet of junk food to five hours of TV a day. Whatever the cause, it's obvious that the more exercise your children get, the better: the greatest gift you as a mother can give them is a head start on a long life full of vigorous physical activity.

Groups are beginning to grow all over the country for families who run together: perhaps the best known is the Pamakid Club of the San Francisco Bay area, which has dozens of families who run together as members. To find out if there is such an organization in your area, and to check on weekly or monthly "fun runs" open to all ages, call your local YMCA or Road Runners Club of America.

Older Women

A recent tabloid featured an article on an eighty-seven-year-old woman who runs a mile every morning. What makes this woman's story even more amazing is that she suffered a heart attack ten years ago, and only began running five years later, at the age of eighty-two! While this woman's case is certainly unusual, it is not unique, and it demonstrates that you can probably begin running at any age, no matter how out of condition you are now.

It is true, however, that older women runners are in the minority. Think about the last time you saw a group of runners. (If you can't remember, you can probably go to your local track and find one.) Chances are there was at least one obviously elderly man on the track, and chances are that when you saw him running, your thoughts were something like "Good for him!" But you probably haven't had similar thoughts about a middle-aged or elderly woman runner, because you probably haven't seen one. The sad fact is that in America there are very few women runners over the age of forty.

This situation will change, of course, as the younger women who are running now grow older and continue to run. But if you're over forty, and you don't have any unusual medical problems, there's no reason why you can't start running now (with your doctor's permission, of course).

According to Dee Howell, who teaches fitness to women at the Rome, New York, YMCA, the major problem she has getting older women to start running is their general unwillingness to spend money on themselves. They won't join the Y; they won't buy a good pair of running shoes. Because these women have been conditioned all their lives to sacrifice for their families— and worse, to feel that their bodies should be hidden—there is a formidable psychological barrier for them to overcome. "But once I get them started," Dee reports, "they become our most dedicated runners. For some of these women, this is the first time they can remember feeling physically good in their whole lives."

One of the best-known distance runners in the country is Miki Gorman, who at the age of forty-two regularly competes in (and wins) marathons all over the country. (She came in *second* among the women in Boston in 1976, with a time of two hours, 52 minutes, and 27 seconds for the more than twenty-six miles. This was much slower than her winning time three years earlier, but she was running in ninety-degree heat.) Though she stands just over five feet and weighs only ninety pounds, Gorman is one of the most outstanding athletes of either sex in the country. She didn't start running till she was in her thirties, and at the age of thirty-five completed one hundred miles on an indoor track in California.

Of course very few women of any age are interested in running a marathon, let alone a hundred miles. But these distances can be achieved by women of any age—and certainly they can begin the running programs described in this book, which involve only six miles of running a week.

There is one further word of caution for women over forty who may be considering a running program. For reasons that aren't completely understood by doctors, older women are particularly prone to the condition known as *osteoporosis*, in which the calcium leaches out of the bones and the bones then become brittle and especially subject to breaking. One of the most important causes of osteoporosis is thought to be inactivity—for example, astronauts have been found to develop osteoporosis after a few days of inactivity in weightless conditions. Although very few studies have been made on osteoporosis and running, some doctors feel that running may help to delay or even prevent osteoporosis in susceptible individuals. If you already have developed this condition, you should use extreme caution in beginning a running program because of the added dangers of falling or of the stress's causing a bone to break. Especially if you are middle-aged or older, it's extremely important to check with your doctor before beginning any sort of exercise program. There is some evidence that a very good diet, including generous intake of calcium (through bone meal), can help to alleviate the condition of osteoporosis, but do check with your doctor.

If you're in reasonably good health, though, you shouldn't have any difficulty following a running program provided you begin slowly and build up gradually. Ruth Baker, a New York actress, began to run for the first time at the age of fifty-four. In addition to a weight loss of twelve pounds, Baker is thrilled with the psychological benefits of running. "It's just wonderful!" she says. "Now I find that the more I run, the more confidence I get. It's really increased my belief in myself. Though I knew it before intellectually, now I have proof that I don't have to be limited because of my age."

In May 1976 Baker entered and completed the Central Park Mini-Marathon, which is ten thousand meters, or a little over six miles. She was so pleased that "I hung my medal for finishing around my neck, as if it were a precious jewel." The following week, she entered and completed a five-mile YMCA race. Baker's husband goes along with her on a bike as she races, and she reports that he's very proud of her. She started running to lose weight and feel better physically, then began running competitively, "not to win, just to prove that I could do it. I wish more older women could know the joys of running. It's too easy to say, 'Hey, I'm too old to do it.' That's *not* true. Nobody should give up because of her age." And as far as age goes, Baker says that running "has made me feel younger than my years, and of course look younger. The only real problem my age seems to cause is that I'm somewhat stiffer than I used to be—but I do yoga exercises and they really help."

If Ruth Baker's story isn't enough to inspire you, then what about the grandmother who "admits only to age sixty-eight," and who runs three times a week in a YMCA program. "I love hot fudge sundaes," she says, "and I figure at my age I have to do something to balance the calories."

Dangers

In the early summer of 1975, Janet Scott was running alone near her home at night when she was attacked by an unknown assailant. The attacker used a heavy concrete block to break every bone in her face, then left her for dead. After a year of expensive and painful reconstructive surgery, Janet Scott is running again. Though this horrible incident could have occurred anywhere, Scott lives in Massachusetts and did her running in a rural area. There have been other rare, isolated reports of runners' being attacked, though most of the victims have been men, probably because more men run. The moral is obvious: there are nuts everywhere, and runners are not immune from attack by them.

But neither are runners more likely to be attacked than other people. In fact, just the opposite may be true. A spokesman for the Police Precinct in Central Park, New York City, reports that it's his experience that runners aren't often robbery victims; most muggers know that runners don't carry anything with them worth stealing, and so tend to leave them alone.

According to the same spokesman, very few women runners are sexually assaulted (as compared to women walking or sitting in the park). He admits he has no statistics to back up this impression, but hasn't personally heard of more than three or four rape cases involving runners in the last eight years, though dozens of rapes are reported in this area every year.

"I guess they figure the girl can outrun them," he says.

All this is not to say that it's necessarily safe to run alone or that you shouldn't take precautions. Obviously you wouldn't go running alone in a city park late at night unless you were trying to devise a new and exciting form of suicide. In Chapter 3, I mentioned my friend who sometimes works late at night. She lives very near Central Park, so when she comes home late, she simply runs in the street alongside the park, and has never been bothered by anyone. "People can see you in the street," she says. "Pedestrians, and doormen, and drivers. But in the park you really are on your own."

In some large cities, police patrol popular running paths at certain hours of the day. The Central Park reservoir, for example, is guarded by a special police patrol from 5:00 to 9:30 P.M., seven days a week, all year long. If there aren't any such patrols in the parks in your city, perhaps you and other runners could get together and ask the police to patrol an area for a certain amount of time.

It's generally considered safer to run alone in the country or suburbs late at night than in the city, but again—Janet Scott was attacked in a rural area. Paula Davenport, who teaches seminars for women runners, runs alone at all hours in the rural area of New Hampshire where she lives. "And when I say all hours, I mean it," she says. "I usually run at 11:00 P.M.—it's my best time; but I've run as late as two in the morning, and I've never been bothered or scared—though maybe I should be. To tell the truth, I'm much more frightened of cars, and I'm always very careful about what I wear— lots of metallic tape and light-colored clothes."

Davenport advises other women to run whenever it feels best, but "if they're very frightened, then they should simply avoid running alone after dark."

If you can't find someone to run with you, your best bet is to run early or join a YMCA. Another solution is to call up your local Y or Road Runners Club and find out if there are scheduled times when runners can go out in a group. Many Y's have "runners' clubs" that schedule regular workouts during the week. As a last resort, of course, you can forget about running outside and find an indoor track.

Whatever your personal solution to possible dangers, just try to remember that your chances of being attacked while running are probably less than at other times. Just as you wouldn't give up your social life and sit paralyzed in your apartment for fear of what might happen out on the street, so you must learn to tune out the possibility that something might happen to you while you are running.

I do know that since I became a runner, I feel somewhat more confident on city streets late at night. Aside from my general overall level of confidence having improved, I also feel (perhaps falsely, but I can't help it) that if someone did try to attack or rob me, I'd have a good chance of being able to outrun him.

Hassles

It's likely that you'll never have to deal with even the threat of attack while running. But you will probably be faced with another kind of problem that, while not dangerous, can be annoying and maddening: lewd comments and whistles from male bystanders and teasing from children (usually also male). This generally happens while you're walking to or from your workout, but you can't always avoid it even if you start running as soon as you leave home.

When I first began running I used to walk several blocks out of my way to avoid obscene comments and disgusting sucking noises from some men at a construction site; now I pay little attention to these distractions—again, I think, because my self-confidence has improved so tremendously. But it's still enough of a novelty to see a woman in running clothes that some men (probably ashamed of their own flabby, overweight condition) feel they have to comment and try to embarrass her. The best advice I can offer is simply to try to tune it out. Don't take it personally—because these men do not see you as a person. My friend Terry takes the opposite approach. If anyone says anything offensive while she's walking to the park to run, she usually shouts back something really filthy in her best nasal Brooklyn voice. This is usually even more of a shock to the man than the sight of a woman dressed for sports, and it usually has the effect of completely shutting him up. My friend Fern, too, prefers to yell back at these boors or simply give them a mute finger. If such a solution doesn't appeal to you, then you'll just have to pretend you don't hear the comments. But you can think smugly to yourself that you're probably in much better physical condition than the man who is annoying you, and that if it came to a head-on contest between you and him, you could outrun him any time.

Children occasionally make fun of or ape the slower runners on a track. This happened to me recently on my local track when some pre-teen-age boys were playing football in the center of the track. I was the only person running, and every time I came near them, they ran out onto the track and huffed and puffed audibly, aping my slow run. I simply ignored them and kept on running. After a while, they quit making fun of me and just watched. Finally, after I had run much farther than I had intended to, I started to leave. One of the boys asked me, almost shyly, how far I had run. "Five miles," I answered casually. "Wow!" said the kid. "That's really good!" Resisting the temptation to say something like "I'm only warming up," I walked home wearing the world's smuggest smile.

Embarrassment

Bodily changes, fear of rape, having and raising children—all these are unique to women and cause problems with running only for women. There is one further factor that affects us more than it does men and that can seriously interfere with starting and maintaining an exercise program: embarrassment.

By now you probably agree that running—if you can get yourself to do it—is indeed just the exercise you have been looking for. But what about the possible embarrassment, the fear of what other people will think when they see your stretch marks and spider veins? These fears stop many women from ever starting an exercise program; they are very real fears and are not to be laughed at. There's a reason for the fears, of course—years of cultural conditioning that have told all of us it's wrong to expose the body, especially an imperfect one, let alone try to improve its condition. To overcome fears of this sort, it helps to realize that your body is a part of you just as important as your hair, face, and fingernails, and that it deserves at least as much attention. And unlike broken fingernails or damaged hair, your body can easily be concealed while you are improving its condition. Tights, sweat suits, and long-sleeved leotards look perfectly natural on a runner, and will help to hide any imperfections that may bother you.

One way to combat embarrassment about your body is to join a group of people who exercise together. The easiest way to find such a group is to join your local YMCA or YWCA. Most Y's have beginners' and intermediate fitness classes which include several minutes of running; in addition, some Y's have active runners' clubs with members at all levels of running. There's nothing wrong with joining a class to do your running: many women find this much easier than disciplining themselves to go out and run on their own every day. I know many dedicated women runners who started out in this sort of class and enjoy the comradeship of running with others more than any other activity.

In any case, the best way for any woman to deal with worries about her body and its shape is to make sure it is in the best and healthiest condition possible—and go on from there. Once you're actually a runner, you'll find that you can accept your body and even be proud of it. Any person feels better knowing that she is in top physical form and looks the best she possibly can. Or as one woman runner summed it up, "I never knew I could do anything at all before—and now suddenly I'm a thin, healthy athlete. I wouldn't give up running for anything in the world."

6

Injuries

DON'T let the title of this chapter scare you. Many runners run injury-free for many long years. And most injuries that do occur are relatively minor and easy to cure. Most important of all, the vast majority of running injuries need never have happened in the first place.

That's right. With running injuries, as with many of life's little disasters, the simplest way to treat them is to prevent them from happening at all. According to Dr. Richard Schuster, one of the country's foremost sports podiatrists, almost *all* running injuries are mechanical in nature; that is, they tend to occur *not* because of outside forces, but because of an inherent weakness that doesn't allow the foot to strike the ground properly. For instance, many runners have one leg that is slightly shorter than the other; while this difference isn't usually visible to the casual observer, it can cause the person's weight to be spread unevenly on the feet or can result in stress on joints and tendons. In most cases, the weakness, whatever it is, can be compensated for by proper exercise, proper equipment and proper running form. Sometimes even very severe injuries can be cured practically overnight by a specially prescribed *orthotic,* a device that fits into your running shoe and compensates for the structural weakness that caused the injury.

Studies show that most running injuries are incurred by those who run more than thirty miles a week. You will probably never be interested in running that much, and certainly not while you are still beginning; but to make sure that you don't injure yourself while you are in training or once you are on your maintenance program, read through this chapter. That way you will know how to prevent common injuries, and if you start getting a pain somewhere which seems excessive for the normal aches and pains of starting a running program, you will know what to do.

The Importance of Warming Up

I hate to be a nag, but I *can't* overemphasize the importance of a proper warm-up. In addition to giving your body a chance to adjust to the stress of exercise, the warm-up will also help to keep you from ever getting injured. Needless to add, you should warm up *every* time you run, not just sometimes. If you are rather pressed for time, it's better to cut a few minutes off your running than to skip your warm-up.

Two of the exercises described in Chapter 4, the hamstring stretcher (page 61) and the calf stretcher (page 61), are excellent for keeping your calf and thigh muscles loose, and thereby preventing a number of injuries in these areas and others. As was mentioned in the section on bent-knee sit-ups (page 66), since running tends to develop your back muscles at the expense of your abdominal muscles, this exercise will help to keep these important muscles in even balance. The tendency of one set of muscles to become relatively overdeveloped in relation to its opposing set can be true of leg muscles as well. If you start to have leg pains, or if you drastically increase your mileage, then you might add the following two strengthening exercises for your shins and upper thigh muscles.

Shin strengthener

Sit on a table high enough to let your legs dangle down without touching the floor. Put a weight over your toes. The easiest way to do this is to get an empty paint bucket or other small bucket and fill it with enough sand (or kitty litter) to make it weigh three to five pounds; then put the handle (wrapped in a towel) over your foot. Now, bend your foot up at the ankle, lifting the weight as you do so. Hold for a few seconds, then relax. Repeat two or three times, then repeat with the other leg. If three to five pounds is too much, start with less sand and work up.

Thigh strengthener

This exercise is done exactly the same way as the shin strengthener, except that instead of bending your foot up, you raise your whole leg from the knee. Lift until the leg is straight, hold for a few seconds, return to starting position. Repeat two or three times, then repeat with the other leg.

What if you should develop an injury in spite of precautions? Well, what you do may depend on the type and extent of the injury. Dr. George Sheehan is said to have remarked that "runners have three natural enemies: dogs, drivers, and doctors." By this Sheehan doesn't mean that you shouldn't see a doctor when necessary, but that very few doctors are knowledgeable in sports medicine. In fact, this whole field is a specialty that is only now beginning to be studied. Until very recently, for example, many injuries were treated by such drastic remedies as complete inactivity, cortisone injections, or surgery—often without resulting improvement. But modern advances in orthopedic medicine now indicate that many injuries, even the most seemingly severe, can be treated mechanically, with shoe inserts and exercise. If you injure yourself, you should see a doctor, of course; but try to find a sports-oriented orthopedist or podiatrist rather than going to your family doctor or gynecologist. A sports-oriented specialist will have access to the latest information and techniques and will probably be able to help you more quickly than a doctor whose specialty lies elsewhere. To find a sports-oriented doctor, call the physical department of your local YMCA or Road Runners Club.

Not all injuries, of course, require medical attention: you can treat many minor ailments yourself. Following is a general guide to common running injuries and suggestions on prevention and first aid for each of them.

Foot Injuries

The foot is the best place to begin any discussion of running injuries, because most problems start with the feet. Even a back or knee problem often turns out to be related to the way your foot is striking the ground, the structure of the foot, or the fit of your shoes. If you take good care of your feet and buy good shoes, and pay prompt attention to any foot problems as soon as they occur, you should prevent yourself from developing more severe problems in your legs, knees or back.

Blisters

Especially common in beginning runners, blisters are one of the most annoying foot injuries you will have to deal with. If you find yourself blistering, first check the inside of the shoe to see if there is a rough place that is rubbing while you run; then check your socks to make sure they are free of holes. To treat the blister, make a small hole in it with a sterile needle and allow the fluid to drain out. The underlying skin will then dry and harden. Cover the blister with a bandage only when you are running or walking in street shoes; at other times leave it uncovered so it will dry. Sometimes wearing thicker socks will help keep the blister from recurring. Many long-distance runners cover their entire feet with Vaseline to reduce friction; though this treatment is a little messy, it is said to be quite effective.

Some runners wear tight-fitting shoes to prevent rubbing and thus eliminate blisters, but this is not generally a good idea. Your feet—and especially your toes—need all the room they can get; it is better to wear looser shoes with an extra pair of socks and, if necessary, to tape the blister-prone area as a matter of course before running.

Calluses

If you have a tendency to get a very large, painful callus in one place—say right below the second toe—then it may be a good idea to check with a podiatrist to make sure there isn't a structural problem causing your foot to strike the ground unevenly. Many calluses are caused by street shoes, however. The most common offenders are shoes that are too large, loose clogs, or any shoe with a hard wooden sole and heel. The best way to remove calluses is to use a pumice stone, which you can buy in any drugstore. Use it in the bathtub, after your feet have soaked for a while, and rub very gently across the dead skin of the callus until it is smooth.

Arch pains

As mentioned in Chapter 3, most running shoes come with good built-in arch supports. If you feel this isn't adequate for your foot, or if you start getting pains in your arches, you might try a Dr. Scholl arch insert (#610). If the pain persists, see a sports podiatrist.

Runner's toe

In the most common form of this affliction, also known as "tennis toe," the area of the toe under the nail turns black. Sometimes the nail itself disintegrates and falls off. Though not always painful, runner's toe is horrifying to look at and unpleasant to contemplate. It's usually caused by crowding of the toes, which then become bruised, particularly when you are running on hard surfaces. The first time I ever had this condition was the first time I ran a six-mile race on asphalt. When I looked at my toe the day after the race, I was convinced I had leprosy at the very least. It took several months for my toenail to grow back to normal and for all the bruising to disappear. The best preventive treatment for runner's toe is to buy looser shoes. If your shoes seem to fit well, then Dr. Richard Schuster recommends cutting two one-half- to one-inch slits lengthwise in the leather on top of your shoe above the toes. Cut through the leather only, not the lining. The extra space the slits provide should help to prevent further bruising and crowding of your toes.

Morton's Foot

This condition, which sounds like a social error, is not an injury but rather a structural weakness in the foot which can lead to injuries of many types. It is one of the most common structural defects found in runners (and in the general population). You can very easily tell whether you have it: just look at your feet. Is your second toe longer than your big toe? If it is, congratulations; you have Morton's Foot.

Dr. George Sheehan describes Morton's Foot as a "throwback" to the days when we still lived in trees and sometimes needed to use our big toes as thumbs. People who have Morton's Foot are unable to spread their weight on their feet properly: much of the weight that is supposed to be borne by the bones of the big toe is shifted instead to the second toe, and it is this shifting and resultant stress that can cause problems. In non-athletes, Morton's Foot seldom if ever causes any discomfort or injury, but once you become a runner (or tennis player or golfer or whatever), the structural weakness, under the stress of increased use of your foot, can lead to many different injuries—in your foot, ankle, knee and back. The most common foot pain caused by Morton's Foot is pain in the ball of the foot or the arch. If you have Morton's Foot and think it is giving you problems, the best thing you can do is see a sports-oriented podiatrist, who will fit you with an orthotic. As you will see, Morton's Foot can cause or aggravate many other problems that seem unrelated to the foot.

Heel pain

This is the third most common complaint of runners and, according to sports podiatrists, the one that responds best and most quickly to treatment. The pain is usually caused by excessive stress on the heelbone itself. This little bone is nearly as round as a golf ball; it is protected by the soft tissue which makes up your heel. But sometimes this tissue breaks down or becomes weakened; when this happens, the bone can develop "spurs," or projections, or become bruised. The best treatment for heel pain is a so-called "heel cup," a device (available in sporting-goods stores) that bunches the soft tissue of the heel around the bone, and particularly under the bone, where cushioning is needed most.

The results of mechanical (that is, non-medical) treatment for running injuries can be swift and dramatic. A middle-aged man I know who had been a runner his entire life suddenly and with no prior warning developed heel pain so severe that he could barely walk, let alone run. His family doctor told him that he might need surgery and that in any case he would never be able to run again. Unwilling to give up his favorite activity, Maury went to a sports podiatrist, who prescribed an orthotic including a heel cup. Within three weeks, Maury was out running one to three miles every morning, without a trace of pain. Not all recoveries from injuries are that rapid, but most can be treated quickly and adequately by doctors who are knowledgeable about the modern approach to sports medicine.

Bump on top of the foot

As far as I know, there is no popular name for this rather common condition, in which a painful, hard bump develops on the top of one or both feet. The pain can sometimes radiate to the toes as well, particularly the big toe. The primary cause of this condition is shoes that are tied too tightly over the bones at the top of the foot. The best way to treat this "runner's bump" is to skip the laces in your shoes directly above the bump. If you should develop this condition, also check your street shoes. Too-tight sandals or any shoe that presses at the point of the bump will only aggravate it.

Ankle Injuries

Pain in ankles

A mild, aching pain in the ankles is fairly common in beginning runners. If the pain persists, or if it starts after you have been running for a few weeks, it may be caused by a foot problem (such as Morton's Foot). Try running on softer surfaces for a while; if that does not help, then see a sports podiatrist.

Sprains

According to Dr. Richard Schuster, sprained ankles are practically unheard of in runners, perhaps because their ankles are strengthened by the exercise of running. The most common cause of sprain in runners is stepping into a hole—usually while running in the dark or running without glasses. If you should develop a sprain see a doctor as soon as possible.

Achilles tendinitis

This troublesome condition is an inflammation of the Achilles tendon, in which the tendon itself becomes tender to the touch and can swell to twice the size of the tendon on the other foot; as a result, both walking and running can be extremely painful. As with many of the injuries described here, Achilles tendinitis is especially common in both runners and tennis players. The cause is usually short, tight calf muscles, which pull excessively and thus strain the Achilles tendon; or weak feet, including Morton's Foot. Achilles tendinitis is often brought on in beginners by overdoing a running program, in either distance or speed; in seasoned runners the cause is usually too much speed work.

The best way to prevent problems with your Achilles tendon is to wear shoes with a good heel support and lift, and—are you ready?—*always* to do warm-ups, especially stretching exercises for the calf muscles.

If you should develop Achilles tendinitis anyway, the main treatments are as follows. Raise the heels of your running shoes: either buy a new pair of shoes with a higher heel, or try putting lifts inside the shoes you now wear (you can cut pads of surgical felt to fit or buy special heel lifts). In addition, slow down your pace while running, and avoid running on hills. After running, apply ice packs to the tendon to reduce swelling and pain. Both before and after running, do stretching exercises for the calf. If you run on a track, try to reverse the direction you usually run in (running always in one direction puts an unequal strain on your feet, ankles and legs). If none of these measures help, then see a sports podiatrist or orthopedist. Although Achilles tendinitis used to be treated primarily by such measures as cortisone shots and surgery, most sports physicians now believe that these measures are seldom if ever necessary.

Lower-Leg Injuries

Aching calf muscles

The main cause of this condition, which is especially common in beginners and in runners who increase their mileage, is overwork. If your calves start bothering you seriously, simply slow down or cut your distance.

Shin splints

This is another of the most common problems of runners, and it is a condition that almost every runner I know, including me, has experienced from time to time. Quite simply, shin splints is pain in the shin area. The pain is most common along the bone in the front or just to the side of the bone. Shin splints is another of those conditions caused or made worse by unequal muscle development: as your calves become stronger, the lifting muscles at the front of your legs become *relatively* weaker. Shin splints is usually brought on in beginning runners by running on hard surfaces or in inadequately cushioned shoes, or by running too fast. For example, you are most likely to develop shin splints the first time you switch from a grass track to the road. A possible contributing factor to shin splints in many cases is a structurally weak foot (such as our old friend, Morton's Foot.)

The best preventives for shin splints should by now be obvious: *always* warm up before you run, particularly concentrating on stretching exercises for your calf muscles, and don't run on hard surfaces. Try to run on grass or a soft track surface, such as Tartan. Other measures which help prevent shin splints include wearing shoes with a good heel lift; avoiding running on hills; never running on your toes; standing more erect while you run (that is, not leaning forward—if you find yourself developing pain in your shins *while* you are running, sometimes improving your posture will help); wearing very thick-soled shoes and good thick socks: doing exercises to strengthen the muscles in the front of your lower legs, such as the "shin strengthener" described on page 105.

If you develop shin splints anyway, put ice packs on the painful area and stop running temporarily—anywhere from a day or two to a week or more. I've had shin splints from time to time, especially whenever I've done a lot of running on asphalt. The pain has never been severe and has always stopped as soon as I started running on a softer surface. Sometimes shin splints can be extremely painful and even incapacitating: one woman I know developed shin pains so severe that it was difficult for her to walk; no matter what kind of surface she ran on, the pain persisted. The primary cause of her shin splints turned out to be inadequate shoes: she had been running in a pair of tennies. When she switched to a good pair of running shoes, the pain went away.

Runner's Knee

Runner's knee is the single most frequent complaint of athletes. Depending on the athlete involved, it is also known as "tennis knee," "football knee," or whatever. The main cause of the condition is an erosion of the cartilage of the kneecap, which prevents the kneecap from riding smoothly in its groove in the thigh bone. The resulting stress causes pain, particularly in the front of the knee along the kneecap.

Runner's knee is almost always brought on because of some structural defect, usually weak feet (Morton's Foot again); one leg's being longer than the other (a condition so common that Dr. Schuster says it's a rarity to see a runner whose legs are the same length); or the short, inflexible calf and thigh muscles that result from running without strengthening the opposing set of muscles. Knee problems can be aggravated by running on uneven surfaces or in inadequate shoes, or by running in one direction only on a banked track.

The cure for runner's knee is to correct the underlying structural problem. Dr. Schuster suggests trying inner soles to cushion your feet. Wear shoes with very thick soles, and of course do stretching exercises for the calf and thigh muscles every time you run. If your knee problems persist, then you should see a sports podiatrist, who will prescribe an orthotic for Morton's Foot, short leg, or whatever the basic problem turns out to be.

If you should develop knee pain *while* running, it may help to consciously turn your feet in and run pigeon-toed for a while; this helps to relieve the twisting that is causing your kneecap to ride over its groove. Many athletes with occasional knee problems wear a "knee brace," an elastic bandage designed to fit over the knee and hold it firm, while still allowing it to bend. You can buy a knee brace in any drugstore for a very few dollars.

Sciatica

This name covers a collection of symptoms all caused by pressure on the sciatic nerve, which runs through the pelvis and into the upper leg. The variety of symptoms produced by this pressure can include pain in the lower back, buttocks, or hips, and numbness in the feet, or toes, or both. The main causes of sciatica are the familiar too-tight thigh muscles and relatively weak abdominal muscles. Not surprisingly, the best preventive and cure for this condition are bent-knee sit-ups to strengthen the abdominal muscles and stretching exercises for the hamstrings.

In addition to the hamstring stretcher on page 61, the yoga half-forward bend (page 68) is also good for stretching the hamstrings.

A note on treating injuries by stretching

Curing an injury by stretching tight muscles sounds too easy to be true; but I can testify from personal experience that in the case of sciatic pain, it works. This is the only sort of problem I have ever had with any regularity, and when it comes on it is *always* after a too-quick (or even skipped) warm-up or when I haven't been doing my sit-ups regularly. As for the too-tight hamstrings, it took me a while to believe that could really be a problem: I have always been able to twist myself into a pretzel fairly easily no matter how out of shape I was. I've found out, though, that this sort of flexibility comes more from relatively loose joints than from loose muscles. As I became a runner, my thigh muscles tightened and shortened relative to my other muscles; though I may seem extremely limber to many people with somewhat tighter joints, as far as my thighs are concerned, at least, I'm practically muscle-bound. The proof of this is the speed with which any back pain goes away as soon as I start concentrating on my stretching exercises.

Serious Injuries

There are many other injuries that can and do occur to runners and other athletes, such as stress fractures (usually caused by putting undue strain on one area till the bone cracks), muscle and tendon tears, and chronic joint conditions. Most of these injuries occur only to runners who train more than thirty miles a week. If you decide to build up to such a training schedule, I strongly suggest that you subscribe to *Runner's World* and buy books on training for long-distance runners; these publications will give you detailed information on how to avoid and treat serious overuse injuries.

Preexisting Injuries

Most of the problems we've been talking about are caused by structural defects (such as one leg's being a little shorter than the other) which you never suspected you had. In addition, some people have preexisting injuries, often caused by car crashes or some sports activity, which they feel may prevent them from running. One of the most common of these is torn knee cartilage. Though sometimes this and other conditions can be so severe that you will never be able to run, and should look to another sport (such as swimming) for your conditioning, even a severe knee problem does not necessarily mean that you can't run.

Bob Glover, the Fitness Director of the West Side YMCA in New York City, was told that he would never run again because he had so badly damaged his knees in sports. After eight years of limited activity, Bob finally went to Dr. Richard Schuster, the pioneering sports podiatrist, and was fitted with an orthotic to minimize the stresses that had helped cause the injury in the first place. Though Bob admits that he still has occasional pain, he trains over one hundred miles per week, and has run as many as three marathons in one month!

Bob's case is extreme, of course, as is the amount of running he likes to do. But his experience shows that it's important not to give up until you have been thoroughly checked out by a sports podiatrist or orthopedist. For most people, there's practically never a reason to let an injury of any sort—from a blister to back pain—keep them from running. And once you're running, if you have good shoes and run sensibly, chances are a blister or two are the only injuries you'll ever get.

7

Everything You Wanted to Ask About Running

As more and more men and women begin running as a way to a healthier and happier life, an increasing number of articles are beginning to appear on the subject. Even so, such articles are still few and far between, and so far they are mostly favorable but limited to such advice as "Sure, go on and run, if your doctor agrees," or "All exercise is good for you, and running is an exercise, so it must be good for you."

But other articles have presented opposing points of view on the benefits of running. Some imply that running can be harmful or that the disadvantages outweigh the advantages. Some even say that running can be dangerous to your health.

This chapter will answer some of the questions raised by the latter sort of article, as well as some of the most common questions that beginning runners (and some seasoned runners) ask about our sport.

Is it true that under some
circumstances running can kill you?

In some circumstances, almost anything can kill you, including your pet parakeet. But yes, people have died while running and as a result of running. In most cases the causes were traffic accidents, heart attacks, and heat strokes. To understand how these deaths occurred, let's take a look at the circumstances one at a time.

1. *Traffic accidents.* Although such tragedies are rare, a significant number of runners have been killed or crippled by cars while they were running. Unfortunately, there is no way anyone, runner or pedestrian, can wholly protect herself from traffic, short of never leaving the house. But you *can* take sensible precautions: wear light-colored clothes at night, run where motorists can clearly see you, be prepared to hit the side of the road in an emergency—and above all, be aware that the danger does exist. Run *defensively,* in other words.

2. *Heart attacks.* In the fifteen years or so that running for health has become increasingly popular, there have been several documented cases of heart attacks that occurred during running or after running. Though such cases are rare, they make headlines. In many if not most of these cases, the runner was a relative beginner trying to go too far or too fast with inadequate training. In other cases, autopsy showed undiagnosed, preexisting heart or blood vessel disease.

To guard against this happening to you, get a thorough checkup by your physician, and if possible take an exercise stress test. Start your running program slowly and build it up gradually. This is especially important if you have a family history of heart disease or a personal history of heart murmur or rheumatic heart disease. Exercise stress tests are not yet widely available, but they are being increasingly offered in hospitals, doctors' offices, and YMCA's (where they are likely to be much less costly). The American Heart Association recommends stress testing to anyone over the age of thirty-five who is beginning a vigorous exercise program.

3. *Heat strokes.* Heat stroke is a much greater danger to runners

than traffic accidents or heart attack; it can kill and has killed beginning runners as well as world-class competitors. The cause of heat stroke is dehydration: when the body's supply of water has been depleted, the body can no longer cool itself off, and its internal temperature begins to rise. The symptoms of heat stroke are a cessation of sweating, a sense of weakness, mental confusion, and finally coma. A common cause of death in heat stroke is heart attack.

The first aid for heat stroke is anything that will immediately cool the victim: ice baths are best. Since the body temperature can rise to as high as 110°F or even higher, prompt treatment is crucial.

Heat stroke is most common in runners who have run very long distances without taking sufficient fluid and who refuse to stop running when they begin to feel ill. (Some marathoners have such a strong competitive urge that it seems they would literally rather die than stop running a particular race.) It is also more common in beginning runners, because seasoned runners are better acclimatized to running and heat, and so are less likely to overdo; but heat stroke can happen to anyone.

The best way to avoid getting heat stroke while running is to drink lots of water, both before and after running; to avoid long distances if you're not used to them, particularly in the heat; if you run long distances, to drink fluids along the route; to avoid running in extremely hot and humid weather; and to stop running immediately if you start to feel weak or faint.

Can running cause damage to the sacroiliac joint?

If you have preexisting damage to your sacroiliac joint—or to any other joints of your body—exercise of any sort will tend to make the damage worse, unless it is exercise designed specifically to strengthen the damaged area. However, damage to any joint is less likely in a body in which the muscles, tendons and ligaments are strong—so running, by toning the muscles all over your body and improving your general condition, will probably help to prevent injury to your sacroiliac and other areas. Women especially are prone to sacroiliac problems; you can help to avoid possible trouble by doing bent-legged sit-ups and concentrating on warm-ups which include stretching of the thigh muscles.

Can running cause a slipped disc?

The discs are soft, fluid-filled cushions between the individual vertebrae which make up your spine. Sometimes, usually during sudden movement or sudden heavy strain, one of these discs ruptures, causing the pain and discomfort associated with "slipped disc" (the medical term is "herniated disc"). There is no medical evidence that running *causes* slipped disc, although this condition can happen occasionally in our sport, as it can in any other activity which involves movement of the back. As with strain on the sacroiliac joint, the evidence indicates that you are less likely to have a slipped disc or any other serious back problem if all of your muscles, tendons and ligaments are strong—these make your back more stable and therefore less liable to injury. So running (along with stretching and warm-up exercises, of course) may help to *prevent* slipped disc and other back injuries.

Does running cause varicose veins or make them worse?

There are two systems of veins in your legs: deep veins and superficial veins. The superficial veins are the ones most likely to become varicose and protrude; anything that encourages blood to remain pooled in your legs makes this condition worse.

Since there is no pump to return blood uphill from your legs to your heart, you are dependent on muscular action and muscle tone to squeeze the deep veins, "milking" the blood upward on its return journey (your veins are equipped with one-way valves, so the blood can't slip back down in the vein). As blood is forced out of the deep veins, the superficial veins drain into them, assuring the continued upward flow of blood. Muscular activity of the legs, then, encourages the return of blood to the heart, while inactivity—anything from a sedentary life to a job which involves a lot of standing and little movement—discourages the return of blood and can in turn encourage the development or worsening of varicose veins.

The best thing you can do for varicose veins, obviously, is to keep moving—and what better way to move than to run three or four times a week? The vigorous action of your leg muscles will improve circulation while you are in the act of running; your improved muscle tone will help move the blood through your veins at other times as well. In fact, some recent studies in Sweden indicate that running seems to discourage the formation of varicose veins in susceptible individuals.

Since people with varicose veins tend to have damage to the valves in their veins, the blood has a tendency to stay pooled in the legs regardless of activity. If this is a problem for you, wear elastic stockings when you run.

Can running cause a fallen uterus?

There is no scientific evidence to support the idea that the uterus can be damaged because of running. On the contrary, as with all the other conditions we've been discussing, improved muscle tone and strength make problems of this sort *less* likely.

Can running cause your breasts to sag prematurely?

Again, there is no evidence to support the theory that running can cause your breasts to sag. While there is also no statistically significant data to prove that running *won't* cause your breasts to sag, no woman runner that I've interviewed has ever reported this to be a problem. The majority of women, in fact, report just the opposite: as their pectoral muscles become stronger, their breasts become firmer and higher, and any sagging previously evident seems to be lessened. In *Women's Running*, Dr. Joan Ullyot points out that the major cause of sagging is stretching of the internal structure of the breast itself, caused by such factors as excess fat and the natural changes of aging. The bouncing movement caused by running will *not* affect this internal structure, but if you are worried about sagging breasts, or find bouncing uncomfortable, wear a very good supportive bra while you run.

Can running bruise your heart or cause it to come loose?

Because the heart is a heavy organ, held in place mainly by thick blood vessels, in some very high-speed impacts, such as car collisions or airplane crashes, the heart can be torn loose and protrude through the crushed chest wall. Because of this, at least one writer feels there's a danger in running of the heart's becoming bruised while "bouncing around" in the chest, if not actually coming loose.

Most doctors believe that this theory is nonsense. If you were able to run at a speed of fifty miles an hour or more, and then came to a sudden stop—say, by crashing into a tree—it's possible that your heart could be damaged in this way. Since the fastest speed that even the very best sprinters in the world can manage for fairly short distances is around *fifteen* miles an hour, heart damage of this sort is probably one of the most remote things any runner has to worry about. Your chances are probably about as good of being hit by a meteorite while you're on your last lap.

Can running cause fallen arches?

If you have a tendency toward weak feet or fallen arches, then, yes, running can make this condition worse. But you can avoid difficulties by wearing good running shoes with an added arch support—either a Dr. Scholl #610 or a specially built orthotic prescribed by a sports podiatrist. Many world-class distance runners routinely insert such devices in their shoes.

There is some evidence, based on the experience of many runners, myself included, that running can help to strengthen weak feet. I was one of the thousands of kids in America who refused to wear my corrective shoes when I was a child, because they were ugly;

partly as a result I grew to adulthood with feet that hurt most of the time and that weren't comfortable in *any* kind of shoes, stylish or not. Since I've been running, all foot pain has completely disappeared, and my arch is stronger and higher than it used to be.

Can exercise cause a woman to develop big leg muscles?

It's true that the more you run, the stronger the muscles in your legs will become. Usually all you'll notice is that the general shape and appearance of your legs have improved, as flabby fat is replaced with firm, smooth muscle. A few women have reported that as their calf muscles have become larger, it has been harder for them to buy tight-fitting boots, though no one has reported an "unsightly" development of muscle mass in the legs. There seems to be a natural limitation to muscle size in women, probably hormonal in origin. For example, women who take weight-lifting classes find that though their strength improves tremendously, they develop none of the protruding, sharply defined muscle mass which appears on male weight lifters.

If you are very worried about the development of large calf muscles, console yourself with the thought that your calves will be firmer and your thighs and ankles slimmer. Slightly larger calves on a pair of trim legs are not a high price to pay for a healthy, fit body.

Will running cure cellulite?

There is no medical evidence that such a thing as "cellulite" exists, but you may be one of many women who have somewhere on their body (usually the abdomen, buttocks, or thighs) that wrinkly, orange-peel–like flab that the media call "cellulite." Whatever it's called, I've had plenty of it in my life; since I've been running most of it has disappeared. In the places where I am completely firm, there is no trace of it; in the places where I'm not, there's still a little. My thighs are completely smooth and firm now, whereas before they were a pocked, blubbery mess.

What happens if you stop running?

The main thing—and the worst thing—that happens if you stop running is that you start to lose your aerobic conditioning and benefits; within four to six weeks almost all conditioning will be gone. When and if you start running again, you will have to start from the very beginning.

Some women put off a running program because they are afraid that if they don't like it and decide to stop, they will gain weight or the muscles they have developed will "turn to fat." If this has been keeping you from running, then you have just lost your last excuse. In the first place, stopping running will *not* necessarily cause you to gain weight. You'll simply have to be a little more careful about what you eat. As a runner, you can eat a tremendous amount of food and not gain an ounce. If you stop, though, you won't be burning as many calories and so of course will have to watch your calorie intake more closely. As for the specter of muscles turning to fat—they will do no such thing. Muscle tissue is one kind of tissue, fat tissue is another; if your muscles are not being exercised, then they will gradually shrink, and their place may be taken by fat—but that is all. Though it's true that you will have less muscle tone because you are doing less exercise, the muscles themselves will remain muscle.

Does running cause charley horses?

"Charley horses"—spasms of the calf muscles—are one of the most painful afflictions known to humanity, and can occur to runners who overdo it—beginners who push too far too fast, and seasoned runners who try for too much speed or distance. It has been my experience, however, and that of other women runners I've talked to, that running seems to cut down the incidence of charley horses and other cramps, such as spasms of the foot muscles.

Is it safe to run if you have chronic respiratory ailments?

This depends on the time of year and the nature of the ailment. The constant movement of running, as well as the rapid flow of air into and out of the lungs, tends to keep the respiratory system clear. As a result, many runners report improvement in chronic bronchitis. Sinus trouble, too, can improve with running, because the movement encourages the sinuses to drain. As for asthma, certainly since running improves your overall conditioning, it can help the general health of any asthma victim; but since asthma attacks can be brought on by exercise, especially in cold weather, caution is advised. If you do have asthma, you can run (with your doctor's advice, of course), but if at any time you begin to develop symptoms of asthma, stop running immediately.

Is it safe to run with a cold?

Some runners keep to their running schedule in all weather, including hurricanes, and in all kinds of physical conditions, probably including mild bubonic plague. Most of the runners I know have run when they had colds; I am among them. Dr. George Sheehan, though, advises laying off for a few days, since he feels that a cold is a sign of a breakdown in your body's defense system. Certainly you should not run if you have a fever or sore throat or some other sign of an infection; if you're feeling really dragged out and sick, why put any more stress on your system? Just take it easy for two or three days, drink lots of juice, and go out again when you're feeling better.

What about running and smoking?

Contrary to popular opinion, you *can* run and smoke (though obviously not at the same time!). I don't need to add, however, that it's not recommended. There's no need to list the many harmful effects of smoking, since we've all memorized them by now, but smoking will definitely interfere with your running performance: you won't be able to run so fast and so far as you would be able to if you didn't smoke, and the running itself won't be so pleasant. This is partly because the carbon monoxide in the smoke takes the place of oxygen in your bloodstream. The whole point of aerobic exercise is to deliver a large volume of oxygen rapidly to all your body tissues, and cigarette smoking directly attacks your aerobic capacity. In addition to the dangers from carbon monoxide, other harmful ingredients in the smoke have a bad effect on your heart and blood vessels.

With all that said, it is true that a number of runners, most of whom would never admit it, do smoke occasionally—from one or two cigarettes a week to ten a day. The more they smoke, obviously, the harder it is for them to run. Smoking more than half a pack a day on a regular basis would probably make running close to impossible for most people.

However, running can help you to stop or substantially cut down on your smoking. In fact, it is extremely common for heavy smokers who begin a running program to discover their need for cigarettes decreasing as they get in better and better condition. It then becomes a simpler matter to quit altogether. The increased calmness that running gives you will help you to get over that jittery feeling during the first few days of cold turkey, and the running itself gives you the feeling of clean lungs, so you won't want to go back to polluting them.

Another very important way that running can help at this traumatic time is by burning calories. Studies show that many smokers don't give up smoking primarily because they are afraid of gaining weight. If you run while you're giving up smoking, and you get the munchies and start eating somewhat more than usual, your weight gain (if any) should be minimal because of the extra calories you are burning. And when you do finally make the break with cigarettes, you will probably be pleasantly surprised to find your running becoming more fun and effortless, as your aerobic capacity automatically increases.

If you simply can't stop smoking, you should continue your running program anyway—the large intake of oxygen probably helps keep your lungs clearer and the aerobic conditioning may help to minimize damage done by the tobacco smoke.

Speaking of pollution . . . Is it safe to run in smog?

Unfortunately, if you live in an urban area, it's almost impossible to get completely away from polluted air. The main contaminants found in polluted city air are sulfur dioxide, which is an irritant gas; smokeshade, the fine particles which give smoke its dark color, and which tend to hang in the air; oxidants of various sorts, which are eye-irritating chemical compounds; and carbon monoxide. The pollutant that is the main concern of runners is carbon monoxide—again, because it directly attacks your aerobic capacity.

Many large cities now issue an "air-pollution index," which indicates the extent of pollution of the air that day: the designations are usually similar to those of New York City—good, acceptable, unsatisfactory, and unhealthy. On days when the rating is "unsatisfactory" you may not wish to run. Your time and speed will probably be a little down, and you'll tend to feel rather blah while you're running. However, most experts think it's probably not harmful to run on such days, or that the benefits of running probably outweigh the disadvantages of breathing in all that dirty air. But if the air rating is "unhealthy," don't run at all. You'll probably be doing yourself more harm than good. (Some runners are so addicted that they run on "unhealthy" days anyway. Recently there was a huge dock fire in my neighborhood—for hours the smoke was so thick that you literally couldn't see across the street. During my usual running time I stayed indoors with my smoke-induced headache, but a friend told me that there were a few people down at the track, four blocks from the fire, running and coughing through the smoke.)

Much of the pollution in cities, particularly the carbon monoxide, is produced by automobiles. Some runners who run alongside roads are going right to the source and getting a concentrated dose of CO whenever they go out for their daily run. If the only time and place you can run is along a roadside during a heavy traffic period, then try to stay at least thirty to fifty feet away from the cars; at this distance, much of the carbon monoxide will have been diluted by air by the time it reaches you.

Is excessive sweating harmful?

Different people vary in their capacity to produce sweat; among my running friends this varies from ladylike little beads of moisture to my veritable Niagara of sweat. The worst danger of sweating a great deal is that of possible dehydration and consequent heat stroke (see page 118)—but this is unlikely unless you run very long distances. In addition, sweat carries with it certain nutrients that must be replaced. If you tend to sweat a great deal, drink a lot of water both before and after you run, and drink fruit and vegetable juices or a special beverage for athletes to replace the needed nutrients.

Excessive sweating can also cause "crotch rot," or an irritated, blistered condition in the inner thighs and groin. This problem can be helped by liberally oiling your inner thighs before you run; dry yourself very thoroughly after you shower and apply medicated powder to help keep the area dry.

Is it all right for runners to wear negative-heel shoes?

According to Dr. Richard Schuster, the sports podiatrist, it's perfectly all right for most people to wear negative-heel shoes if they wish—*but not to run in!* Some people have such short calf muscles or Achilles tendons that this type of shoe can be painful to walk in. Before you spend your money, Dr. Schuster advises you to walk around indoors barefoot for at least half an hour. If your feet and legs don't bother you, then you can probably wear negative-heel shoes, but get used to them gradually.

Because the negative-heel shoe pulls on the calf muscles, it can help to stretch out too-tight muscles, but be very careful. There is evidence that these shoes can aggravate Achilles tendinitis in people who already have a tendency to this condition.

8

Sticking with It

So now you're a runner. You have embarked on a program that will improve your appearance, your health, and your state of mind. You are beginning to know the joys as well as the occasional pains of athletic endeavor. You are probably starting to recognize some of the other runners in the gym or park or track where you take your workouts. Perhaps you have already started to lose weight, sleep better, and feel better physically. Psychologically, you probably feel great about yourself. You've set out to do something important for yourself, and you're doing it. Every week you're noticing improvement in your energy level and endurance. Every week, or nearly so, you find you can run a little farther. You're making real progress.

But what next? Once you've reached your maintenance program, is that all there is to it? Just going out and running three or four times a week, like clockwork, day in and day out, ad infinitum, or worse—ad boredom?

Surprisingly, this is the time when many runners quit—after they have achieved their goal of basic fitness, and perhaps have stuck with it for months, or even a year or more. Most of these runners feel better than they ever have felt in their lives. But still, after a few weeks, months, or even longer, they stop running.

Why should this be? Why would someone give up something that she enjoys and that she knows affects her life in a positive way? Generally, it's because the runner's attitude has changed. When you first start out running, you have a definite goal. Perhaps it's to achieve the maintenance level and be able to actually run a mile and a half without stopping. Perhaps your goal is to lose twenty pounds, or to do something about the insomnia that's been making you impossible to live with. Whatever it is, eventually—and sometimes in a surprisingly short time—you reach that goal.

For a while, you can continue on sheer momentum. For the first few weeks or even months, you can still get a great kick out of being able to run one and a half miles continuously, or perhaps you decide you want to run more, and continually set new goals for yourself. But even that can wear thin after a while. By the time you're running, say, ten miles six times a week, the daily workout may settle into a boring routine unless you continue to have a positive attitude toward running.

I'm not suggesting that running will or even should always be the high point of your day (though it often will be), or that you should always look forward to it the way you do to a night at the ballet. But consciously and unconsciously, from the very beginning, you should do everything you can to make running a natural and deeply ingrained part of your life—a habit, in other words. Once running has become such a habit, you'll scarcely ever think, "Oh, darn, I've got to go out and run." Instead, you'll just go out and do it, because it's as natural to you as breathing.

So that you will want to continue running now that you've started, this chapter offers hints from other runners on ways to stick with it beyond the initial training period. Not all the suggestions will necessarily work for you, and you may have others of your own. But read them through, especially if you're feeling discouraged, and remember—just as nobody is a born guitarist, so nobody is a born runner. But you can become a natural, habitual runner, if you really want to.

How to Make Running a Part of Your Life

Joe Henderson, editor of *Runner's World*, believes that most runners—particularly health-oriented runners—who quit do so because they look upon running as a nasty medicine to be forced down. This attitude is especially common in women runners, because so few women have pleasant memories of physical activity going back to childhood. To such women, running is something to be gotten over with, like a visit to the dentist or the yearly Pap smear: "All right, I'm doing it because I know it's good for me. But I hate every minute of it."

Such feelings are understandable, particularly if you feel rushed and as if there's simply not enough time to fit everything you want or need to do into a given day. If this is your attitude toward running, or if you ever find yourself starting to feel this way, then my first suggestion to you is: slow down. Look at the hours in your day and the way you are spending them. Chances are there is very little time that you have set aside for *you*—that is, for your own physical and emotional needs. You should try to look on running as part of such a time. Henderson suggests that you set aside a special time just for yourself, say an hour and a half a few times a week. Even the busiest women can manage one and a half hours three times a week. Running will fit into that time—but so will other things. Take your time dressing for the track. When you are through warming up and running, take a long, leisurely bath or shower. Do your nails. Soak in scented bath oil in a tub. Have a glass of wine. Pamper yourself. And most important of all—don't let anyone or anything take that hour away from you. No matter how pressed for time you may feel, keep reminding yourself that if you maintain a regular running program, you will sleep less and have more energy, so in the long run you will actually end up with more time for anything you want to do.

On the other hand, don't go to the opposite extreme and become a slave to your routine. Maybe you can't always make your three or four hours a week on the same day or at the same time. If you can't do it, if you have to skip or postpone a workout, that's all right, too. But do try to maintain that time you've set aside for yourself—only for yourself. If you just can't go out and run, then do something that you really feel like doing. Read a magazine. Paint a picture. Sit and daydream. But know that this time is *yours* and yours alone. And if you have to skip your workout from time to time, above all don't feel guilty. After all, running is something that you are going to do for the rest of your life; one workout more or less won't make very much difference in a lifetime of running.

Another way to avoid becoming a slave to your routine while still maintaining that routine is consciously to vary some elements in it from time to time. For example, if you always run on Monday, Wednesday and Friday, try running on Monday, Tuesday and Thursday. If you always run a mile and a half, try running two miles—or just run for fifteen to twenty minutes without paying any attention to the distance. If you always run on a track, try running though city streets, or on a beach, or along a quiet country road. If you always run in the mornings, try running in the afternoon. I'm not suggesting here that you should vary one or more elements in your routine every single time you go out and run, of course, but if you ever find yourself getting stale—and we all do—then do change these things, at least occasionally. You'll be surprised how much interest they'll add to your running routine.

As you continue to run, and particularly as you get to know other runners, you may fall into another trap that causes some runners to give up—comparing yourself with other runners in a negative way. A little comparison, in the form of mild, friendly competition, is fine; in fact, it can sometimes spur you on to greater effort, as my friend Fern and I find when we run together. But it can also be depressing to

see the same person pass you time after time on the track, or to see
her always looking cool and refreshed after her run while you feel and
look like a piece of six-day-old parsley. The way to avoid this trap is
simple: just don't compare yourself with other people. My friend
Nancy runs four miles five times a week. Sometimes I wish I could
run as much as she does, even though deep down I know that I don't
really want to expend that much time or energy. In other words,
twenty miles a week is right for her and makes her feel best, and it's
what she chooses to do. Around ten or twelve miles a week is right for
me and makes me feel best. On the other hand, I run somewhat faster
than she does, and she has remarked that she would like to have my
speed; but whenever she tries to push herself, her ankles start to
hurt, and she no longer enjoys her workout. The moral? Run at the
speed and the distance that are right for *you*. You're not in a race—
except against time—and you will win that race by being as young
and healthy as possible through all your years, as long as you
continue to run.

One other factor that sometimes causes runners to drop out of a
successful running program is the problem of going stale. As I
mentioned in Chapter 4, everyone has occasional bad days—when
you go out to the park and find that *walking* a block, let alone running
a mile, is exhausting and boring and depressing, when even after
you're into your workout you don't think you can put your foot in front
of you one more time. Those days come to all runners, even serious
competitive runners, but those days always pass and are succeeded
by equally positive days. But sometimes they don't vanish right
away. Sometimes you will have several days or even weeks of feeling
blah, of being unable to achieve your normal time or distance, and
you can't imagine what's wrong with you. During those times the
temptation can be great just to give up, to decide that there must be a
better way to spend your time than dragging your tired body around a
track. Don't give in to that temptation. Instead, just slow your pace
down, run as much as you can without exhausting yourself, and tell
yourself that things will get better. And sooner or later, in a matter of
days or weeks, they will.

If you keep in mind that things always get better, that as your weeks, months, and years of running go by you will continue to feel better (and certainly look better) than other women your age—in other words, if you keep a positive attitude about your running—you should have little trouble in making running a basic part of your life. That's the most important thing: your attitude. Maintaining a positive attitude about anything isn't always easy, but there are many strategies that other runners use to keep themselves going, and you may find one or more of them helpful.

Keep a Record

Most runners keep some sort of record of their mileage or times or both. Even though it's a fairly simple matter to remember in any given week how far you have run, it can give you a real sense of accomplishment to look back on the last several weeks or months and see how much distance you have covered. Some runners, in addition, keep a record of the temperature, how they felt, and other data for each workout; you may or may not want to go into so much detail, but having such a record can be very helpful to runners preparing for competition.

Some gyms have wall charts where runners can record their times and distances and informally compare themselves with other runners. I always write down in my pocket diary as well as at the Y how far I run each week. When I added up my mileage for my first year, I was surprised and a little smug—but that was nothing compared to the thrill I felt when I discovered that I had the eighth highest number of miles of all the hundreds of new runners at the YMCA!

Another way a record can help is to keep your running in perspective if you have a particularly busy week or two (the in-laws are visiting, you have to grade final exams, and the Labrador retriever has just had eight puppies). If you've been keeping a record of your running—or in this case, most probably non-running—you will be able to keep yourself from going too long between runs. Instead of wondering, "Now when did I last run? Thursday? Friday? A week ago Tuesday?" you can just look it up, and if it's been four or more days, you know it's time to let something else go and get out for at least a short run.

Run to Wichita

Another device often used by runners, particularly those primarily interested in mileage rather than amount of time run, is to mark progress on a map. This is actually a variant of the diary technique.

To use this technique, get a very good, detailed road map of the U.S. or a state, or any place in the world you are interested in, which has roads marked off in miles or kilometers. Then, starting at one point—your home town, say (or Addis Ababa)—and using pins or a magic marker, start recording your progress. Did you ever wonder how long it would take you to run from Salem, Oregon, to Miami, Ohio? Well, you can easily find out if you mark your progress on a map. One married couple I know tried this method with an interesting twist: starting at opposite ends of the country (she in New York City and he in Los Angeles), they started running to meet in the center of the country. The winner, who would take the other out to dinner, was to be determined by how far east or west they met. They haven't come close to meeting yet, but I'm betting on her. (I think the reunion will take place somewhere slightly west of St. Louis, even though they're actually doing all their running in New Jersey.)

Make Your Friends Your Allies

One woman runner I know insists that she has absolutely no self-discipline and that even though she loves to run, she would never be able to stick to her program if it weren't for her friends. "I meet them on a fixed schedule," she says, "three times a week. In addition, I try to run one more time on my own, though sometimes

I don't make it. But I *always* manage to meet my running friends—I guess because I know they're counting on me, plus I can't face what they'd say if I missed one or two workouts."

Your friends don't actually have to run with you to be of help. Paula Davenport, who teaches running seminars in New Hampshire, has an informal agreement with her husband: "If I start dragging around and I'm not really in the mood to go out and run, he pushes me out the door. Needless to say, I do the same for him."

Even if your friends or relatives aren't sympathetic toward your running, they can be unconscious allies in making running a part of your life. My friend Fern's brother has never been able to understand why his little sister would want to run, even though he's told her how good she looks since she became a runner. But she reports that he's a great help in getting her to run, particularly on Sundays when she feels a little lazy. "We almost always get together for a while on Sunday afternoon," she says. "And Stephan always says something sarcastic about my running—like 'How many hundred miles did you run this week?' Well, usually I don't think anything about it. But last Sunday I just stayed in bed and didn't run, and when Stephan asked me later how far I'd run, and I said I hadn't even been outside, I could see he was shocked. That's when I realized that I'd really built up an expectation in him. Stephan and so many of my friends now see me as a runner that I feel I'm letting them down if I don't run."

A corollary to making your friends your allies is what I like to call "social running"—an extension of the idea of getting together with friends on a fixed schedule. Remember, the goal of running is to run at a pace at which you can comfortably carry on a conversation. Many women find that they have some very rewarding and interesting social interactions running this way. Social running can be done with many different people, of course—you can meet friends regularly, you can join a running club or do most of your running with a class at the Y, or you can make friends with other runners on the track or out in the park where you usually run. I've met a lot of interesting people that way, and have enjoyed running alongside a stranger, getting to know her or him in a way that isn't really possible

in any other kind of social setting. On my local track, many of the
runners gather after they run and just sit around and look at the
sunset and discuss running and life in general. One woman I know
has met several men there whom she later dated. Runners share a
bond: only another runner can truly understand the frustrations and
pains of running—and the joys and satisfactions.

Read About Running

I am one of those persons who want to know everything—to the
very last detail—about anything that interests them. My friend Nan,
on the other hand, is interested only in being able to master basic
techniques. Once she has them down, she is satisfied. You are
probably somewhere in between, but I think that most runners do
enjoy reading about running and finding out about other runners.
This can be especially useful if you've been going through a stale
spell—or if you've been sick or on vacation and are having trouble
getting motivated to run. If this happens to you, just read about
running for a while. Buy a general sports magazine and look up
articles on runners in general and women runners in particular.
Reread parts of this book. Subscribe to *Runner's World* magazine.
Buy a book on long-distance runners or running. Even read a novel,
such as *Marathon Man*, by William Goldman, which features running.

For most runners I know, this method of revitalizing interest is
almost sure-fire. I use it myself from time to time, saving particular
articles in *Runner's World* for those times when I feel my general
interest flagging.

Compete

For many runners, particularly goal-oriented men runners, one of
the best ways to stick with running is to get into frequent competitive

racing. A growing number of women, too, are enjoying this way of staying in shape, which will be discussed fully in Chapter 11.

Off Days

Once running is truly a part of your life, you will find it easy to stick with in the long run: your body and mind simply won't let you go too many days without a workout. But what about particular days—those occasional times when you aren't quite motivated? In other words, how do you get yourself to go out and run on any given day when you aren't in the mood? Well, each woman's answer is as individual as she is, but here are some of the tricks that other women runners have used to make themselves run when they don't feel like it; try the ones that appeal to you the next time you have an off day.

Method #1: Don't Run

"I used to spend about half my life feeling guilty about things," says one woman runner I questioned. "I decided early in the game not to add running to that list. So on the days when I'm really not in the mood, I just don't run. I know that I'll feel more like it the next day, so I take a nap or go to a movie, and then the next day I'm usually much more ready to go out and hit the track. Come to think of it—maybe it's because I feel guilty about not running the day before!"

Another woman, who maintains that she usually runs by using "sheer will power," also admits that even will power can break down. "Sometimes I feel I just can't do it," she says simply, "and so I don't."

Method #2: Give Yourself a Pep Talk

This is probably the method most used by women runners to get themselves out on the road. It is usually done one of three ways, and most of the runners I know use one or more of them more or less often.

How does it work? Just tell yourself, as Karen I. puts it, "I know how much better I'll feel afterward." This is how I usually get myself to run if I'm not in the mood, or if I'm feeling particularly dragged out and tired. It probably won't work for beginning runners, because you haven't yet felt all the benefits of running—but after you've been running for several weeks, you'll know from experience how great you feel at the end of the workout, how energized, wide awake and relaxed. Even if you are very tired some days and want to sleep instead of working out—unless your problem is total exhaustion caused by a lot of sleepless nights—you will probably feel more refreshed after a run than you would after a nap. "I just talk to myself," says a woman who runs on my local track. "I say, 'Mary, you'll feel better when you're through.' And you know what? I always do."

The flip side of this strategy is to tell yourself how bad (or guilty) you will feel if you *don't* run. "I tell myself that if I don't run, I'll get fat again," says a woman who lost twenty pounds running. "And to reinforce it, I keep an old picture of myself in a size 16 dress. On days when I'm *really* not in the mood, I drag out the picture and look at it—and usually there's no more problem."

The final variation on this theme is consciously to think about the long-term benefits of running. "I just remind myself how much better off I am now," says my friend Janet. "I have greater endurance, better circulation, firmer and stronger legs, clearer skin. . . . And I know that to keep those benefits I have to keep on running. So, even though I might not feel like it sometimes, I usually stick to my schedule."

"I just look in the mirror," says another woman. "I probably shouldn't admit it, but I love the way my body looks now. I used to be ashamed of my legs, but now I think they look great in shorts—and I usually run in shorts. I met my present boyfriend out on the track, and he told me he thought I was in as good shape as women ten years younger than I. Any time I don't feel like running, I just think about that and about him—and put on my track shoes."

Method #3: Fool Yourself

Many women have devised ways of tricking themselves into running. The most common of these is often used by Lena T., who runs between twenty and thirty miles a week. "I tell myself I'll go out for a walk at least or just a very short run to get some fresh air. Then once I get going I keep on. And those not-in-the-mood days often turn out to be the better ones. I often end up running farther and faster than usual."

"I go to the Y when I'm not in the mood," says an older woman runner. "Then, once I'm in the class, it's too late to back out!"

Another woman uses a similar approach, but adds, "I try not to even think about it; I just start running slowly, always with the idea that if I don't feel better, I'll go back in. And if after a few minutes I'm still not in the mood, then I do stop. But I never feel guilty, because at least I made the effort."

Method #4: Bribe Yourself

Often you can get yourself into the mood to run by rewarding yourself: tell yourself that after the run you deserve to go shopping, or to a movie, or to eat a really disgusting sundae. My friend Fern prefers to think of this form of motivation as a "bribe" rather than a reward: "When I'm running mornings, I tell myself, 'If you get up and run, then you can have such and such tonight.' Usually it's something special to eat—and usually it works."

"When I'm having trouble running," says another friend, "especially if it's been going on for days, sometimes buying a new T-shirt or leotard helps. Somehow, having something new to run in is motivation to go out and actually run in it."

I've probably used all of these tricks and techniques at least occasionally. Another one that I find works especially well for me is to call up a friend to run with me. Somehow, having someone to work out with can really help, both in starting and in finishing the run.

Aside from the subtle level of competition between you and the friend, you can really psych each other up to continue, no matter how dragged out either of you is feeling.

Finishing a Run

Sometimes the problem isn't so much one of getting out and running as of finishing a given run. From time to time, through fatigue or boredom or the approach of your period, or for seemingly no reason at all, you get out on the road and start to run, and you suddenly think, "What am I doing here?"

Often the best thing to do in a situation like that is to give up, go in, and try again the next day. But sometimes you can get yourself to go on anyway. The first way to ensure that you will finish the run you have in mind is *always* to run at a comfortable pace. This pace may vary greatly from day to day, week to week, or even within a given run. For every conditioned runner, there is a pace, usually quite slow, at which she feels she can continue to run almost indefinitely. Find this "cruising" pace and maintain it—then you will know that there's no reason for that awful feeling that "I can't go on."

Another way to continue your run is to try not to have an end in sight. In other words, even though you *know* you're planning to run a mile and a half, try not to think about that. Just decide that you're going to run for a while. The first few minutes of a run can often be deceptive, anyway: you'll start out feeling really unenthusiastic, and then suddenly, after five minutes or so, you begin to feel energized, as if you could run forever. So run for a little while, as least, and then, if you're still feeling blah, stop and go inside. Above all, again, *don't feel guilty*. The important thing is that you are a lifelong runner, even if you can't make it on this particular day. Try to remember that anything is better than nothing. Or as Joe Henderson puts it in his column in *Runner's World:* "Even a trickle of running adds something to the pool of fitness."

9

Running It Off

IT is a fact that you seldom see a fat runner. Go out to the park or to your gym—most of the people you see zipping around the track are slender, if not actually skinny. The very few overweight runners you do see are probably running precisely in order to lose weight. Even if you have a lifelong tendency toward gaining weight, or an occasional insatiable craving for chocolate-covered cherries, once you become a runner, excessive weight will probably never again be a serious problem for you (although you may experience an occasional weight gain of a few pounds, particularly if you stop running for a while or go on a real binge).

Though not everyone is seriously overweight, far too many Americans are at least a little heavier than they should be (about half of all men and a third of all women). Even women who measure out svelte on those weight charts may still be too fat—either because all of their weight is in unconditioned flab or because they are figuring their weight for a heavy-boned frame, when they actually have a small one. What about you? How much should you weigh to look and feel your best? Well, physical fitness experts and life insurance statisticians are continually revising the figures downward. There is a growing body of evidence that thinner people do lead longer and healthier lives. You probably already know whether you should lose weight, but here's an easy way to figure the approximate weight that is best for your height and bone structure: first, give yourself ninety-five pounds for five feet of height, then add five pounds for each inch over five feet (or subtract five pounds for each inch under five feet). Now add five pounds for large bone structure, or subtract five pounds for small bone structure. In addition, take off one pound for each year of age under twenty-five. This figure should give you an approximate weight that is right for you. As long as you are within five pounds of that weight on either side, you probably weigh about what you should. But remember, chances are that you are better off weighing a little *less* than a little *more*.

All of us have a tendency to gain weight as we grow older. This is not only because most older people become less active physically and thus burn fewer calories, but also because the body's metabolism tends to slow down with age. For each year after age twenty-five, in fact, you need about ten fewer calories a day than when you were younger. Ten calories a day may not seem much, but if you continue the eating habits you had when you were younger, those calories can add up over the years to a few excess pounds. In fact, by the time you reach age thirty-five, you need one hundred fewer calories a day than you did at age twenty-five. One hundred calories translates to a glass of milk, an orange or three cookies, which you can easily overlook.

It's this tendency of the body to slow down as we get older, as well as the sedentary life style of most Americans and a national diet high in sugar and fat, that leads millions of Americans to spend billions of dollars on books about dieting, on dieting clubs and magazines, and on special low- or no-calorie diet "foods."

There is an easier way to lose weight and keep it off, and that is to make running a regular part of your life. Not only will running help you to lose weight; it will also help you to keep it off. Most of the diet clubs and books, as well as diet doctors, advise that the best way to keep weight down is to permanently change your eating habits, as well as your exercise habits. Running can help you with both. It can help you to change the way you eat, while still enabling you to eat more than the average sedentary person your age. And since running will be a regular part of your life, these changes should be permanent.

How Running Can Help You Lose Weight

In a 1973 survey of its readers, *Runner's World* magazine found that of the runners who responded, almost two-thirds had lost weight since they had started running. Of the sample, eleven percent lost less than ten pounds, twenty-five percent lost from ten to twenty pounds, fourteen percent lost from twenty to thirty pounds, and fifteen percent lost more than thirty pounds.

Many women runners I have talked with have reported similar loss of weight—I lost about ten pounds during my first year of running, without consciously trying to lose. Some of the women who have lost *were* trying to lose, of course, but for many others, it just seemed to happen. Many overweight women are still reluctant to begin a running program because they are afraid the exercise will so stimulate their appetites that they will be tempted to eat even more. Though it is true that moderate, short-term exercise (such as an afternoon of yard work) does tend to have this appetite-stimulating effect, vigorous exercise over a sustained period of time seems to have the *opposite* effect. The act of running shunts blood away from your digestive organs and into your legs, heart and lungs; the exercise raises your blood-sugar level as well. The result is that you are not hungry for quite a while after running. I have felt this effect myself many times: I go out to run, thinking, "Wow, I'm starved. I'll never get through this!" After about five minutes I'm no longer hungry, and when I'm through running, eating is almost always the farthest thing from my mind. A half-hour or more after the exercise, of course, your blood-sugar level returns to normal, and you will probably feel hungry—but *you probably won't feel any hungrier than you would have if you hadn't run*. If you can avoid the psychological temptation to overeat because of all the hard work you have just done, you probably won't eat any more than the amount of food that is customary for you.

Running can help you to lose weight in other ways as well. The first of these has to do with the obvious fact that the act of running burns extra calories; in addition, since maintaining a regular running program will make you more calm and relaxed, you may be at least somewhat less inclined toward compulsive eating, if that is your problem. Finally, some doctors believe that vigorous exercise such as running seems to speed up intestinal transit time—in other words, the food spends less time in your stomach and intestines, so there is less time for calories to be absorbed.

I used to believe that my metabolism had somehow altered once I became a runner, because I noticed that I could eat a great deal more rich food than previously, even when I wasn't running regularly—on a short vacation, for instance. Now I believe that the effect I observed was probably due to the increase in intestinal transit time. Other runners have reported the same thing—that they seem to be able to eat whatever they want now; but they and I may have somewhat smaller appetites than most people. If you are a compulsive eater who constantly craves ice cream, rich sauces, and marbled steaks, then running is going to have to be combined with diet and will power, and you'll just have to face the fact that you'll probably never in your whole life be able to eat all you want with impunity.

Losing on the Run

I must underline here that running can only *help* you to lose weight. To lose at all, as you know, you must use up more calories than you take in. Though running will certainly burn calories, the process of significant weight loss will be slow unless you run very long distances or cut down on the amount of food you consume.

I have a friend in California who is a sometime-runner. That is, he follows his program faithfully for months or even a couple of years. Then he starts to drop off and either doesn't run at all or runs only occasionally. This same friend has a weight problem—but it only bothers him when he isn't running regularly. The last time I saw him he was running sporadically, as well as attending a weight-watching club. His club met every Tuesday night, and part of the routine was a weigh-in: members who had gained over the week were fined money and subjected to criticism from other members. While my friend practically never stuck to his diet during the week, he still managed to avoid paying the fine for overeating. He did this by fasting and then running three miles every Tuesday just before the club meeting; the amount of water he lost in sweat usually kept his weight below the level that would have meant a fine. Of course, he was always hungry and very thirsty at the meetings—and he wasn't fooling anyone, not even himself. The moral? Exercise alone won't do it, or won't do it quickly.

In other words, calories *do* count, even if you're a runner; and even if you run twenty miles a day, you still can't eat unlimited amounts of food (although at twenty miles a day, the amount you could eat might seem unlimited, since you would burn up over two thousand calories just by the running alone).

However, researchers are coming to the conclusion that the process of weight loss is accelerated when dieting and vigorous exercise are *combined*. In order consciously to lose weight while you are running, there is more than one approach you can follow, taking advantage of the different ways in which running can help you to lose. The first and probably simplest method is to get a good low-calorie diet from your doctor or from a weight-losing club (though of course you should never begin a diet of any sort without first checking with your doctor). Follow this diet while you begin the running program: the combination of fewer calories and more exercise to burn up the calories you are taking in should result in a fairly rapid loss of weight.

By "rapid" I mean a steady loss of one or at most two pounds a week. While it is true that it's possible to lose five, ten, or even more pounds in a few days on some kinds of crash diets, these diets are not good for you, and further, this is not the sort of weight loss that you can easily maintain.

As for the diet you follow—if your doctor agrees, try to include plenty of raw and cooked vegetables. Recent evidence indicates that a high-residue diet tends to speed up intestinal transit time, as well as to bind certain fats so that the body can't absorb them. (But if you are planning to participate in a race or to undertake long-distance running, you should avoid high-residue foods for a few days before the run).

If your doctor has no objections, you might try combining your diet with an occasional fast of a day or more (though you probably shouldn't run on the days you are actually fasting). I have several friends who have fasted with some success, particularly at the beginning of a calorie-restricted diet.

If you don't want to bother with a structured diet but would rather continue to eat what you wish, you can calculate a calorie-reduction plan on your own. If you devise your diet, do include foods from all the basic food groups, including fish, meat, eggs, nuts and beans; green and yellow vegetables; grains; and other fruits and vegetables. While it is true that you would lose weight on a restricted-calorie diet which consisted of nothing but limited amounts of cake and potato chips, you would not feel particularly well and might in addition damage your health. To put together your own low-calorie reduction plan requires only a little basic knowledge and a little arithmetic.

First, your basic piece of information is that one pound of fat equals about 3,500 stored calories. In order to lose that pound of fat, you have to create a deficit of 3,500 calories—through exercise, cutting down on food, or both. Since running a mile uses approximately 80-120 calories, you would have to run between thirty-five and fifty miles to lose that pound of fat through exercise alone. That's not quite so bad as it sounds, though. If you run six miles a week, then in a month you run twenty-four and in two months forty-eight. If all else remains constant, you will tend to lose at least a pound every two months (forty-eight miles will easily burn up one pound of fat). Over a period of a year, that means a loss of from six to ten pounds without conscious effort.

That figure of 80-120 calories burned each mile is only approximate. For simplicity, you can figure about one hundred calories a mile and not be too far off. I mentioned earlier in this book that the rate at which a calorie is burned is fairly constant no matter how fast the pace of the mile; the difference in calories used in running a five-minute mile or a ten-minute mile amounts to less than the number of calories in a cube of sugar—*for people of the same weight.* The number of calories burned every mile differs more for people of different weights than for those with different paces. In other words, if you're heavy you'll tend to burn more calories each mile than your thinner friends, no matter how fast you or they run—although this difference won't be very great.

If you don't have very much weight to lose, and want to lose it with a minimum of discomfort, you might try a program which includes cutting out, say, two hundred calories a day (roughly equivalent to one tablespoon of mayonnaise and three cookies) and running your maintenance program of six miles a week. In two weeks you will have a deficit of around four thousand calories, or well over a pound. Of course you can accelerate the weight loss by cutting out more calories or running more miles a week, or both. A more rapid weight loss would result from cutting out four hundred calories a day and running seven miles a week. Such a program would result in a total deficit of 3,500 calories a week—or one pound.

And remember that as you're dieting, you will start to *look* much thinner long before you reach your actual weight goal. Almost all runners report a loss of inches in the waist, arms, hips, thighs—whether or not there is a corresponding weight loss. Even if your diet seems to be producing minimal results, you will almost certainly be in a smaller dress size within a very few weeks or months as your weight is redistributed and fatty tissue is replaced with lean muscle, which weighs more than fat but takes up less space.

Even though combining running and a diet can make the process of weight loss easier, for most women any sort of diet is no fun. But you can make it easier by taking advantage of some of the natural benefits of running. For example, try to schedule your workout for a time just before your biggest meal of the day. That way you almost certainly won't be very hungry, and will find it much easier to eat less. Your appetite may be so small, in fact, that you can easily save part of the meal to eat later, as a snack, without adding any extra calories.

Another way to combine running with dieting is to run *instead* of eating a meal. This may sound like the worst form of self-torture, but I've known several men and women who have scheduled their running for lunchtime. Not only does the exercise provide a relaxing break from work, but afterwards they're not tempted to eat a heavy, greasy lunch. If you don't want to skip lunch altogether, you will probably be satisfied with a salad and juice or coffee.

If you're a seasoned dieter, you already know that weight loss is not a smooth, continuous process, but rather proceeds with occasional stops at new weight plateaus. Running will not help you avoid those annoying plateaus where you just can't seem to start losing again, but running *can* help you get off them. If your weight-loss progress seems halted after a while, the best thing to do is to increase the amount that you are running—just slightly—while reducing the amount you are eating—again, just slightly. (For example, run three extra miles a week and cut out five hundred extra calories a week.) Within a very few days you should begin losing again as rapidly as you like.

Once you have lost the desired number of pounds and have

reached a new weight plateau (while continuing to run), you can gradually start to reintroduce some of your favorite high-calorie foods. In fact, you can even, within reason, make up for occasional binges by extra running.

By now you may be thinking, "All this sounds great, except for one thing. How can I possibly run while dieting? I'm usually too weak to walk, let alone run." If this is bothering you, cheer up. In the first place, once you have started a running program, you will probably have so much increased energy that exercise won't be a strain. In the second place, running does *not* require a high-calorie diet. The Tarahumara Indians of Mexico, who regularly run one- and two-hundred-mile relay races in connection with religious ceremonies, subsist on what most Americans would consider a starvation diet, consisting primarily of corn and beans, with a little meat only once or twice a year. Not only are the Tarahumaras among the world's greatest runners, but they live long and very healthy lives.

Dr. Ernst van Aaken believes that everyone should take in fewer than one thousand calories a day. Although his position is controversial and considered by many experts to be extreme, van Aaken maintains the Spartan diet he advocates is not only healthful but also conducive to better running. "Run hungry" is his watchword.

While you probably wouldn't want to go to the extreme of the Tarahumara Indians, or to run as hungry as Dr. van Aaken recommends, you may find that combining running and dieting is the easiest way you have ever found both to lose weight and to keep it off.

And this is true no matter how much weight you have to lose.

Virginia Murling, a forty-four-year-old housewife from Rome, New York, began running at her local YMCA as part of a reducing plan. What makes her story unusual is that the plan's aim was to lose two hundred pounds! Murling lost the bulk of the weight at a weight-losing clinic which emphasized balanced meals and calorie reduction; then she joined the Y and began exercising, running, and swimming.

"The exercise helped enormously," she reports, "but I still believe that controlling calorie intake is the most important thing." Murling has now been running for a year and a half, and while she usually runs three miles at a time, she has run as far as eight miles continuously. Since she began running she has dropped another twenty pounds, but even more important, her heart, which formerly beat at over 200 strokes a minute after exercise, now "cruises" at a rate of 135 beats a minute while she runs.

Her appearance, too, has improved. "Even though I still have a way to go," she says, "I've lost a lot more inches than would have seemed possible. I lost four or five inches off my waist, neck and arms. And of course the muscle tone is better all over my body."

Murling emphasizes that it may be harder for heavy women to get up the nerve to start running or join a class. "You just don't want to go out in shorts and a T-shirt and let people see you. That's why it's probably best for very heavy women to start with some sort of class. Even though you're convinced everyone in the class will be looking at you, they won't be. They're too busy concentrating on their own exercise."

After a while, Murling began running outdoors. "It's my nature not to get too bothered about things," she admits. "Besides, I thought up little strategies to keep people from embarrassing me. For instance, sometimes I run by the local high school. When I see some teen-agers up ahead who look as if they're going to say something, I speak first. I ask them what time it is."

Rather than ridicule, Murling has received a great deal of encouragement, from her friends and family as well as from strangers who have seen her running. "One man whom I used to pass while he worked in his yard always used to stare at me as I ran by," she reports. "I couldn't imagine what he was thinking. But after I'd been running about six months, he suddenly smiled and said, 'My goodness, I certainly can see the difference in you.' "

When Murling first began her exercise class, she found that one of her biggest problems was finding running clothes that fit. She advises other heavy women to just go and buy exercise clothing in the men's department. "You'll soon be in a smaller size, anyway," she says. Another important piece of advice for overweight women, particularly those with large breasts, is *not* to wear a long-line bra while running, but rather a very good, short supportive bra. "When I first started I wore a long-line to smooth my shape," Murling says, "and I nearly smothered. Not only that, but when I got home I saw that the ribs in the bra had cut deep grooves into my body which didn't go away for several hours." Although the instructor at the Y discouraged it, Murling wore elastic underwear for the first few months of exercising so she wouldn't "shake so much." Even so, she found that the most painful area was her rear end. As the exercise instructor explained, "The biggest part is the one that's going to hurt the most."

Today Virginia Murling is nearing her ideal weight, and she wouldn't give up running for anything. Two years ago she ran in the Mini-Marathon, and she plans to continue running as long as she lives. The exercise has helped her to maintain her new eating pattern, she says, and besides, she feels better than she ever felt in her life.

Perhaps Murling's feelings about running and diet, as well as those of many other formerly heavy women, can be summed up by a woman runner who lost twelve pounds running, but who still loves sweets: "Let's face it," she says. "It's still a struggle. But if I didn't run, it would be hopeless!"

Other Exercise

As Virginia Murling's experience shows, a good, well-balanced but low-calorie diet is essential for permanent weight loss of more than a few pounds. But her experience also points out that additional exercise beyond running can help to speed up your reducing program. Though she gets the bulk of her exercise running, Murling also swims and does calisthenics. From my own experience, I know that whenever I have stuck with an exercise class on a regular basis for more than two weeks (in addition to my running), I have lost weight, even when I didn't want to. If you don't feel you have time to join a calisthenics class, or if you are already enrolled in one, there are many other ways to increase the amount of exercise you do without spending much extra time. The most obvious one is to walk more—to and from work, say. Once you are a runner, such walking will be easier and will tire your feet less while it helps to burn even more calories. You can also do calisthenics on your own, play active sports such as tennis, or dance, which is another good way to burn up a few extra calories.

What about weight *gain* while running? To be perfectly honest, running is not a good way to gain weight, although anyone who starts running, fat or thin, will redistribute the weight she has in a way that is more desirable for her general build. I know that very thin women sometimes suffer a great deal of embarrassment because of their extreme slenderness and that it can be extremely difficult for them to buy clothes that fit. Even so, most experts feel that a tendency toward excessive thinness is *not* a good excuse not to run: all the health benefits of running will help you look and feel healthier and better no matter what your weight. One of the top distance runners in the country, Miki Gorman, has great difficulty gaining and maintaining weight: during the 1976 Boston Marathon she lost so much weight that she had to wrap her body in a towel so that she could fit into the new evening gown she had bought for the post-race festivities. While many news reporters made light of this, I'm sure Gorman suffered acute embarrassment—and yet she would never dream of giving up running. In short, if you feel you are too thin, try to count your blessings and run anyway, remembering that running will still help you to look the best possible—for *you*.

Nutrition and the Athlete

Whether or not you are trying to lose weight, you may wonder whether your nutritional needs will change once you begin running on a regular basis. The answer to this question is *yes and no*.

Certainly, since you will burn more calories than you used to, you can increase your consumption of calories without gaining, although this may not be desirable, particularly if you wish to lose weight.

But what about extra protein? After all, the image of the athlete has always been that of a steak-and-eggs eater who needs large amounts of high-protein lean red meat. Is there any truth to this image? Well, all of us need protein in order to carry on the basic processes of life—but according to *Runner's World,* studies indicate that athletes have no unusual need for protein beyond the amounts required by more sedentary people of the same weight. You may obtain that protein from many sources other than meat: from eggs, milk, fish; from beans, nuts, seeds, grains (in the proper combinations)—in short, even a vegetarian diet is compatible with running as long as the foods are balanced properly.

Do runners need any extra vitamins and minerals? Again, there is no clear-cut answer to this question; the experts are pretty much divided, some maintaining that any athlete should take supplements and others just as certain that we get all the nutrients we need in our food, assuming a well-balanced diet. Beyond this, what is known for sure is that some water-soluble vitamins and some minerals are lost in the sweat, so if you run long distances and sweat a lot, it makes sense to drink fruit and vegetable juices to replace these nutrients. As for other supplements, it's an open question. A *Runner's World* survey indicates that most runners do take some supplements, the most popular being vitamins E and C; but be careful and ask your doctor's advice before adding anything out of the ordinary to your diet. I personally take a wide variety of food supplements but of course can't make any recommendations to other runners. As long as you don't take unusually large amounts of any vitamin, you probably have nothing to lose but money, and you may gain in added health.

Perhaps the best nutritional advice of all, for dieters, vitamin-poppers, and average eaters, is that given by Dr. George Sheehan, with his three rules for wise and healthy eating: "1. Eat foods that agree with you. 2. Avoid foods that disagree with you. 3. Don't go to bed mad."

10

What to
Think About
While Running

"**I** can see that running's good for you—I mean, there's a difference in how you look, all right, but how can you keep doing it? Isn't it boring?"

"Running? Oh, I've thought of taking it up, but it's too tedious."

Do these comments sound familiar? They are to me, and to most other experienced runners, for this is the image that most people have of running: that it must be terribly boring. Even *The New Yorker*, in an article otherwise favorable to running, reported that our sport is one of the dullest possible ways to keep in shape.

Once you have become an experienced runner, of course, you know that running is no such thing, that it is as absorbing and intriguing as any other worthwhile activity, but of course there is a germ of truth in the idea that you can become bored while running. The daily workout is *not* always fun and interesting, and sometimes the time spent doing it seems to drag. But can you name any other activity of which this isn't occasionally true?

If you start out with the idea that running will be boring, it probably will be for you. But this need not be so. For just as running can benefit your body physically in untold ways, so it can uplift your mind and spirit. Nobody knows yet exactly how running works all its miracles of relaxation, strength and energy, but I'm sure that at least some of these effects come from the calming influence running can have on your thought processes, if you allow it to. After all, what other time do you have to let your mind go where it will, or control it, or just let it observe the things around you with the freedom that you have during your daily run? I know that running has made a profound difference in my own peace of mind, and, wondering what went through other women runners' minds while they ran, I decided to ask them.

I was not surprised to find that the dozens of women I talked with all go through similar thought processes, and that we fill our minds according to certain patterns. Most important and perhaps least surprising, nearly everyone agreed that any feelings of boredom become less frequent and less intense the longer you have been running.

In fact, you can almost tell how long someone has been running by her answer to the question "What do you think about while you are running?"

"How soon I can stop," says Helen Y. When I first heard her answer I had to laugh, but then I realized that she had fallen into the common beginners' mistake of worrying about the distance or time she was "supposed" to cover while on the road. Running for her was not yet a natural, joyful part of her life, although she was already happy about the physical benefits of sleeping better and losing inches all over her body. Helen's answer made more sense when I learned that she had been running only a month and was still overly concerned with the physical processes of her run.

Aside from this slight caveat against thinking too much about how far you are running or still have to run, you can think about anything at all during your workout—including some things that you don't usually consider at any other time.

"It's my happy time . . ."

Ruth Baker, the actress, looks upon running as "a happy time, my positive-thinking time." Sometimes, in fact, she runs an extra day if she's feeling a little low. "If I'm depressed, running somehow always brings me out of it," she says. "I don't know why; maybe it's all the oxygen circulating in my body. But if there's something on my mind, or I'm down in the dumps, I just turn my mind loose on happy thoughts. I think about an upcoming vacation, for example, or visits from friends. This is really the only time I have to think about those things, because I'm so busy the rest of the day."

Many other women like to fantasize while they run. "I free-associate," says one woman. "I just let anything come into my mind, and then build fantasies around that. Or sometimes I think about the men on the track. Wondering what they're like, why they run, how their bodies would feel to touch . . ."

"Men runners drive me crazy," says Kitty L. "I mean, most of them are in such great shape, and they're running in tight shorts and no shirts. . . . There's one man in particular whom I see quite often. In my mind he's been my lover a dozen times. The funny thing is, I usually don't fantasize about men at other times. There's just something about running that gets my juices flowing."

For most women there seems to be something about running that gives them permission to think about otherwise taboo or unrealistic topics. Things may not always work out the way we want in life, but we all know they can work out in our daydreams. "Things have been pretty rough at work," reports a young buyer-trainee for a department store. "Since I run at night, work is usually the main thing on my mind. I start playing over what happened that day and then fantasizing about it. In my head I'm perfect—I don't make any mistakes. In my favorite fantasy, the president of the company comes in and sees how brilliant I am and immediately promotes me to head of a whole department. Of course I know it's not going to happen that way, but it's nice to think about."

Many women think about food while they're running, especially those who are trying to lose weight. "My whole life I've fantasized about food," says Mary E. "And I really let my imagination go wild when I'm running, because I know it's safe. I mean, I'm practically never hungry when I finish, so there isn't much danger I'll go out and buy something really gross."

"I plan what I'm going to have for dinner," says another woman who's watching her weight. "Sometimes I go out to the track with the idea of later having some terrifically rich meal, usually featuring pasta, butter and cream. But after running for fifteen minutes or so, I've usually talked myself into a cantaloupe and some cottage cheese."

For most women, pleasant thoughts just seem to come naturally during a good run. "I think about how beautiful nature is," says my friend Elizabeth. "I love smelling the air, especially when there are flowers and trees around, and looking at the sky, the clouds, shadows on the grass. I think I notice these things much more when I'm running than when I'm not."

Plans

Since running is essentially a free time for your mind, a time when it isn't occupied with anything other than directing your feet, many women take advantage of it to plan the day's or week's activities.

"Whenever I'm going to have a dinner party," says Edna C., "I go out and run an extra amount a few days before. I figure out my menu, and usually even manage to plan what order to prepare and serve things in."

"I go through a mental inventory of the house," reports a busy young mother. "I review what we're out of, what can wait till next week, and so on, and then when I'm through running, I just go to the market in my running clothes."

My friend Terry, who works and goes to school, usually plans her evening while she runs. "I'm usually too tired to even think when I go out after work," she reports. "But after a while I relax and start thinking about what I have left to do that evening. Somehow, it doesn't seem so overwhelming any more, and I can usually put things in some kind of working order."

Of course every woman runner, no matter where her mind is wandering, keeps at least a part of her consciousness on the running itself. It is a good idea to at least check yourself from time to time to make sure you are relaxed and not falling into any bad habits. Some women, particularly those who are training for competition, devote much of their mental energy to perfecting their stride. There comes a point at which you can do this more or less automatically, without cutting into your planning or daydreaming. "I used to think about the effort it took to run," reports a young woman who's been running for six months, "but lately I've been trying more and more to relax and get running off my mind, and it seems to be working. The funny thing is, I think I'm running better."

Many women, especially beginners, sometimes find themselves getting bored anyway, probably because their bodies are still not accustomed to the work of running. These women devise mental games to fill their minds while they run. The most common of these is to "sing" songs, either aloud or in their heads. "My favorites are Bob Dylan songs," says Emily B. "I play the guitar, and I find that running is a good time to memorize long lyrics. Also, by really concentrating on the song, I usually find that the lyrics end up meaning more to me."

"I use songs sometimes if the time seems to be passing slowly," says a woman who's been running three years. "Since I run on a track, I like to pick songs that seem to last a certain number of laps. For instance, at the pace I run, 'Me and Bobby McGee' is exactly three laps. When I have about three laps to go, if I'm feeling bored, I just start playing the song in my head, and I know that as soon as it's over, I'm through running."

"If I have to keep track of laps, I make up rhymes to do it," says another woman. "Simple things, like 'One, one, run for fun.' "

Some women who are mathematically inclined like to count and make computations of laps or blocks. "I go through all sorts of mathematical tricks based on my running," says Lillian W. "I'm constantly refiguring percentages of a mile, depending on how many blocks I have to go, or computing the number of calories I'm burning. Sometimes I make a special point of counting the cars or people I saw on my last run. I guess it all gives me a sense of continuity."

A Time to Create

The majority of women runners, at least sometimes, find that running can be a time of great creativity, a time to solve problems, artistic and otherwise.

"I make choices," says Nina Kuscsik, one of the country's top distance runners. "I've planned a term paper, picked out wallpaper, even chosen the godparents for one of my children."

"I find the answers to the problems of the day," says Helen M., a seamstress. "Sometimes I work out complex sewing problems."

Many artistically inclined women find that while they are running they can write poems, find the opening paragraph for a story or article, or plan how a painting or sculpture should be approached.

There are many documented stories of scientists having worked on problems for a long period of time and then suddenly having the solutions come to them in the form of a dream; for example, the structure of DNA, the building block of life, was discovered in that way. Something like this process seems to occur in running. I know that often when I've had a problem—either personal or having to do with work—if I've kept it in the back of my mind during my run, by the end of the run the answer suddenly comes to me. In fact, the idea for this book came to me one day while I was running and thinking about the other people on the track and wondering what *they* were thinking.

"Transcendental" Running

Meditation in various forms has attracted millions of people all over the world. The devotees of this discipline praise it for clearing their minds, for enabling them to concentrate and relax better, and for helping them to realize a myriad of other benefits, both mental and physical.

Some experts believe that there may be certain similarities between meditation and running. For one thing, both stress erect posture; calm, even breathing; and concentration. For another, both allow the mind to disengage itself from its usual daily tasks.

In Transcendental Meditation, the goal of the meditation period is to become unaware of, to "transcend," yourself and the passage of time. When this goal is achieved, the meditator leaves the session with renewed physical energy, feeling mentally refreshed and relaxed. Sometimes the same sort of thing seems to happen in running. I call it "transcendental" running, because when it happens, you feel as if you have transcended the usual physical limitations of time and of your body, and you finish your run with a profound feeling of calm, both physical and mental. Most of the women runners I have talked with have experienced these feelings from time to time; it is most common in women who run long distances (six or more miles) often.

But even if you don't always "transcend" yourself, running can still be a time of meditation or mental relaxation for you. In fact, there are certain steps you can take to achieve this relaxation consciously. The first of these is to try to let your mind go blank for part of your run: try not to think about anything at all. This may sound like a contradiction—something like "try not to think about a chartreuse elephant." But it can be done. I find that when my mind empties out in this manner, as it does only occasionally and for limited periods, not only is the run more enjoyable, but anything that was bothering me before the run seems much easier to deal with. Another way to work on achieving this state of mental relaxation is to concentrate on something very simple. For instance, many women say yoga mantras to themselves or repeat "Om" with every exhalation.

"I think about my breathing," reports Karen B. "I mean, I really concentrate on it, thinking in-out, in-out, and then the first thing I know I start to go blank and I feel I'm fusing with nature."

"When I start running," says another woman, "at first I think about the running itself, or work or school, and then about the things around me, and gradually I withdraw and find a kind of peace that's inside of me."

With practice, you can learn to control your mind far more than you think, and running is a good time to practice this discipline. For instance, if you have a tendency, as I do, to dwell sometimes on unpleasant thoughts, even when you're running, set aside a part of the run—say two laps—when you will *not* think about unpleasant things. Pay attention to your thoughts, and whenever you find your mind wandering back to the depressing subject, focus on something else—the sky, the other runners around you, your breathing, or, ideally, nothing at all. With practice you can extend this time of mental control, and you will find it extremely refreshing.

Meditation, relaxation . . . whatever you call it, this time of running can be one of the most spiritually rewarding parts of your day. Or as my friend Barbara puts it, "It's my prayer time. As I run along the river and look at the sky and clouds, I feel that I know what people have always meant when they talk about God."

11

Competition

$\mathbf{A}$S recently as 1970, women athletes had to get special written permission from the American Athletic Union to compete in running events longer than five miles. This despite the fact that for years many women had been running unofficially in races as long as the marathon (more than twenty-six miles) and even longer. The Olympics themselves were strictly male until 1928, although athletic events especially for women had been organized sporadically in different parts of the world. The main reasons for the exclusion of women from long-distance running events seem to have been apathy on the part of officials who didn't want to do more work and the popular idea that women either are not competitive or are too weak and fragile to do anything more strenuous than run around a quarter-mile track a couple of times.

The treatment of women runners began to change in the early

seventies, mostly as a result of the courage and determination of a few women. Though women had run unofficially in the Boston Marathon for years (along with many men who just wanted the experience of running at Boston), it wasn't until Kathrine Switzer entered the race officially under the name of K. Switzer (later to have an outraged official try to rip her number from her chest) that racing organizers and the news media began to realize not only that women were serious about their desire to compete but that they could actually run very long distances with good times and without collapsing in shock at the end of the race.

Today women are allowed to compete in most distance events in this country under AAU sanction (up to fifty miles), though most long-distance running events in the Olympics are still closed to us (the longest official distance in 1980 will be 3,000 meters, about two and a half miles, unless some drastic changes are made). This is partly because women in many other parts of the world are still bound by traditional roles and so are not pushing in their countries for more official races for women. However, many other women, particularly in America and Europe, are lobbying for more and longer events. In addition, more new races for women only are beginning to open up, and others will be added as more of us show that we wish to have a chance to compete regularly in a wide variety of distances.

Women's competitive running has come a long way in this country in the short time since K. Switzer entered the 1967 Boston Marathon. In 1972, Boston itself was finally opened to women: there were twelve official entries. By 1976, the number had gone up to seventy-five women—all of whom had to qualify by running in a previous official marathon with a certified time of less than three and one half hours (which works out to around an eight-minute mile for twenty-six continuous miles!). The Mini-Marathon in New York City has become one of the most prestigious races in the country for runners of either sex; in 1976, over four hundred women entered, from all corners of the United States and from many foreign countries. Other

Road Runners- and YMCA-sponsored races have more and more women entrants with each passing month. The women who enter these races are of all ages and occupations: they range from middle-aged housewives with several children (or grandchildren) to teen-age and even younger girls who run on their school teams.

Why Compete?

The idea of running a race with dozens of spectators watching may seem too scary and strenuous even to consider, but before you definitely decide that competition isn't for you, take a closer look at it. For one thing, as Nina Kuscsik points out, you don't have to think of it as *competition*. Think of it as running together with other people, "to show off what you can do." Only a tiny minority of most entrants in any race have any thought of actually winning or even placing well; the main thing is to get out and finish, just to prove to yourself that you can do it. Many runners compete regularly—several times a month or more—without ever having won so much as a medal. But over the months they see their own best times improve; they feel better physically as they stay in competitive form; and they enjoy the socializing that usually goes on before and after (and sometimes during) a race.

Most runners do compete from time to time anyway, even if they aren't aware that they do. If you keep a record of your times and distances, you are, in a sense, competing with yourself. If you're not actually trying to better your distance or time, you're making sure you don't slip, which is a way of pushing yourself to excellence. If you run with friends occasionally, you already know that this type of running is competition on its lowest level. Perhaps you're not trying to beat the friend or prove you can run farther and faster than she can, but I know that whenever I run with someone, I never want to be the first one to suggest stopping!

Competition can also make running easier to stick with over the long haul—the race as a goal can keep you interested in your workouts even on days when you aren't really in the mood to run. Runners who run six or more miles at a time—either regularly in training or in occasional races—report that they get what amounts to a natural high from the running.

The final argument in favor of competitive running, at least once in a while, is that it can be a lot of fun. In the first place, the racer is truly part of a group effort: it can be exhilarating to know that you're about to run five miles along with dozens or even hundreds of other people. If you do finish well—or in some races, if you finish at all—you will be awarded a medal or certificate, and that can give your self-confidence a real boost. Especially for someone who has never been athletic or goal-oriented in her life, it can be quite a thrill to see that medal with the little ribbons and know that you won it because of something you achieved through physical strength and mental determination.

Earning a trophy is not all that difficult, anyway, especially while the sport of women's distance running is still in its infancy. In many races special prizes are given out to contestants in different categories—for example, oldest person in the race, youngest, and so on. In the Mini-Marathon there is a special award for the woman who most improves her time over the previous year, as well as a small medal for each finisher. And in almost all races, there are different awards based on the age groups of the participants: under fifteen, over thirty, over forty, over fifty, etc.

How do you find a race to run in? Well, the easiest way is to check with your local YMCA or Road Runners Club. Many of these sponsor regular runs of varying distances, from two miles to ten or more. In addition, some local groups sponsor "fun runs." Official *Runner's World*–sponsored fun runs are increasing in popularity all over the country; your Road Runners Club or Y will be able to tell you whether such races are scheduled in your area.

A fun run is a very good way for any woman to *start* competition. The idea of fun running is that dozens of runners of all levels of training run a preselected distance over a marked and measured course. The distances usually range from one half mile to six miles, with optional distances in between. One reason a fun run is such a good way to begin competitive running is that the competitive aspect of the sport is played down, giving beginners a chance to get used to running set distances with other runners. The races are as short or as long as you want them to be—you choose your own distance before you start (many fun-runners start at the shortest distances and then work up to six miles). Best of all, there is no bureaucracy to deal with—no sign-up sheets or entry fees, no necessity to show up two hours before the run begins. Many fun-runners help each other with tips on better running form and preparation, and you will be able to meet some of the best runners in your area at these runs. If you enter an official *Runner's World* fun run, in addition to savoring the excitement of running with other health-oriented runners, you will receive an official certificate, color-coded to show the distance you ran. Since there are no official results in a fun run, it doesn't matter how fast or slow you run, but you will be given an accurate time for your distance as soon as you cross the finish line.

The Mini-Marathon

Almost every woman runner I've spoken to has either run in the Mini or plans to run in it at some future time. Many, many women, including me, got their first competitive running experience in this prestigious race.

The Mini-Marathon (which is sponsored by Road Runners, the West Side YMCA, and Arno Niemand) is run along a road that circles New York's Central Park, over a beautiful course that includes hills, lakes and trees. The distance is 6.2 miles, or 10 kilometers. The most important feature of the Mini, of course, is that it is for women only, one of the very few events in the world for long distances.

The Mini was started in 1972 as part of a promotion campaign for a ladies' shaving cream. The first year there were fewer than one hundred entries, and the press tended to make light of the whole thing. The name didn't really help, implying that women can run only a "mini" distance compared to men. But the name "Mini-Marathon" has stuck because it is catchy, much more so than such alternatives as "Central Park Women's Ten-Thousand-Meter Run." By 1976, there were 427 entrants in the Mini; and the press was no longer making fun of those women. Several course records have been set by winners of the Mini, and women from all over the world now come to New York to compete. At the most recent Mini, in fact, I heard some men complaining about how unfair it was that they should be excluded from running. Who knows? Maybe someday in the future some male equivalent of K. Switzer will sign up in advance, and the truth won't be known until he shows up at the starting line . . . to have his number ripped off by irate officials!

If you don't live in or near New York, of course, you probably won't be able to experience running in the Mini-Marathon (though you could always schedule a vacation to New York during the first two weeks of May). But there are undoubtedly some races in your area open to women, if not for women only. Kathrine Switzer and other top runners urge all women runners to organize races of their own, particularly at distances of five thousand to ten thousand meters: only as more women prove that they are serious about running, even if not necessarily about winning, will the Olympic Committee and other sports organizations take women runners seriously.

Competition is not for everyone, of course, and you may find after your first race that you never want to race again, or you may never want to race at all. I personally don't particularly enjoy running competitively, though I enter a very few races every year just to prove to myself that I can do it—that is, that I can finish. But I never try to push my speed and have never finished with what could be called by any stretch of the imagination a good time. I do know, however, that the satisfactions I've gained from the few races I've run have been invaluable, and I am very grateful to have had these experiences. For that reason, I urge you to enter some sort of race at least once—even if just a two-mile fun run—to see what you can do. You may find, much to your surprise, that you have a real competitive streak within you, and end up aiming for Boston!

Running Your First Race

Whatever your first race—the Mini-Marathon, a full marathon, or a half-mile fun run—there are certain steps you should take to prepare yourself so that your run will be as pleasant and productive as possible.

First of all, how do you know when you're ready to run a race? The best guideline is to ask yourself two questions. First, have you been running regularly at distances that are close to those of the race? In other words, if the longest distance you have ever run is two miles, then you probably shouldn't enter or expect to finish a six-mile event. Second, have you been running for a period of time long enough to give you a general idea of what your limits are, both in speed and in distance? If not, you may get caught up in the excitement of the race and push yourself too hard—to exhaustion or injury. On the other hand, don't go to the other extreme and become *too* cautious, or you'll probably never be able to psych yourself up to race. Most women are very nervous on entering a race for the first time, yet find much to their surprise that it was far easier and more enjoyable than they had anticipated.

Training

Depending on the length of your first race, you should try to spend some time for a few weeks beforehand preparing for it. You probably won't want to try to win your first race, or even to place particularly well; most of the women I know who have run competitively for the first time ran with only one goal in mind—to finish, either running continuously or walking as little as possible.

The rule of thumb for most distance races is that you should run twice the distance of the race itself *weekly* for several weeks before the race. In other words, if you are planning to enter a five-mile race, then you should run at least ten miles every week (in five two-mile segments, say) for several weeks beforehand. This training should ensure that you will be able to finish the race without exhausting yourself.

For women who race to win, or to finish with very good times, some speed work is advised as well. Most experts now believe that around five percent of your total mileage should be at faster than "cruising" speed. So if you run two miles during every workout, about one tenth of a mile should be at a speed which pushes you a little. If you do most of your running on a track, it's easiest to set aside, say, one lap out of every twenty to run fast; if you run for twenty minutes a day, try to run fast one minute out of that period.

In addition to running regularly (at least three or four times a week), competitive runners should, according to most experts, include some rest as part of their training program. Either don't run at all on some days or schedule alternate workouts to be very slow and easy.

Women who run very long distances competitively train at what seems to be a killing pace. Jacki Hansen, for example, who won the 1976 Boston Marathon (for women), trains by running four hours a day, with a one-hour workout in the morning and two or three hours in the afternoon. Most women don't have the time or the drive to train so intensively, of course, but workouts of at least fifty miles per week are necessary for athletes who want to become world-class competitors.

If possible, try to run on the race course at least once before any race. This is important so that there won't be any surprises; also, if the course is on asphalt or is very hilly, it's a good idea to have at least some experience with that sort of surface before you run on it seriously.

Since your goal in your first race is probably just to *finish*, it is very important for you to know how to pace yourself so as not to become tired too early in the race. In order to do this, you have to know what your limits are: how far you can run, at what pace you are most comfortable, how much you can push yourself before you start to feel tired. The best time to find these things out, of course, is during training. Nina Kuscsik advises beginning competitors to go out on a track with a stopwatch a few days before the race and time themselves over varying distances—to get an idea of their cruising speed, then to see how fast they can sprint short distances. "It is extremely important to have an idea of your own limits," she stresses.

During the training period prior to a race it is also important— perhaps more so than at other times—to do stretching exercises and other warm-ups, and to concentrate on building strength in areas where you are relatively weak, such as your stomach muscles. In addition, yoga exercises can be very helpful, especially if you've been running longer distances than you are used to.

Food, drink, supplements

There's no need to plan any unusual diet while you are training for a race (see section on nutrition, page 153). On the *day* of the race, though, what you eat—or what you don't eat—is more important. Although common sense might seem to dictate a high-protein breakfast such as steak and eggs, most serious competitors prefer to run on a relatively empty stomach—the last thing any runner wants is to have to go to the bathroom in the middle of a race!

Many runners limit their breakfast to coffee and juice on the day of a race; if you feel you absolutely must have something, then try a light meal of some easy-to-digest food such as yogurt several hours before starting time. And of course increase your intake of fluids before the race.

There is no need to take salt tablets or extra salt in any form at all before a race; in fact, Kenneth Cooper and other researchers are beginning to believe that excessive intake of salt can be harmful, since most of us get plenty of salt just in the food we eat. Cooper believes that drinking extra fluids is far more important than increasing salt.

If you begin to race or to read about racing with any regularity, you will probably hear the term "carbohydrate loading." This is a method of eating before long-distance races which, according to its advocates, increases maximum performance. What it involves is, first, a very long run (90 minutes or more), followed by three days of a low-starch, high-protein diet that empties the system of stored sugar; this is in turn followed by a very high carbohydrate (starch and sugar) diet for three days before the race. This regimen increases the amount of stored glycogen in the muscle tissues—a sugar burned to give energy during the race. Most serious marathoners do practice carbohydrate loading, but there is no reason for anyone running shorter distances at a slow pace to try it.

Whatever you eat during training, remember that it is extremely important to run with a relatively empty stomach and colon; to aid in this it is a good idea to avoid high-residue foods (grains, fibrous vegetables) for a few days before the race.

What to wear

There's no need to wear anything other than your usual running clothes during a race, but if you are going to be running outdoors at longer than your usual distance, you might want to add a hat or suntan lotion to protect yourself from sunburn. Also, for long distances or hard surfaces, an extra pair of socks may help prevent blisters and "runner's toe."

During the race

Once that gun goes off at the starting line, you're on your way!

A mistake many beginners make at this time is to run as fast as they can; these are the same women who usually spend a large part of the end of the race walking. Start out at a *comfortable* pace. If you feel good and want to pick up the pace a little after you've been running for a while, fine—but give yourself a few minutes at least to settle in and get an idea of how you feel. Good days and bad days do not happen only in training; they can occur during races. It is very easy to forget this matter of pacing and become overconfident. Even though your goal in a race may be only to finish, if only as the last runner, somehow the experience of being behind the starting line with dozens or perhaps hundreds of other runners makes you want to go out and show everybody. But if you're not ready for it—don't try.

If it's your first race, it's possible that at some point you will feel tired and tempted to give up. How do you keep yourself going? Nina Kuscsik advises you to keep in your mind the knowledge that "you have a choice. You can quit or keep going. Just remember that—as long as you know you can always quit sometime, then that's often enough to keep you going to the finish line."

Another method that often helps is to run with a friend or with a group of friends. Many women do this in the Mini-Marathon and find that the group effort keeps them all from getting discouraged. (If you plan to race alone, though, Kuscsik stresses that it's important to train alone as well, at least part of the time; otherwise it may be hard to keep yourself going alone.)

A hurdler I know advises that if you are feeling very fatigued toward the end of the race, you should concentrate on keeping your eyes wide open and your head up—even try smiling. Somehow an alert expression can keep you from submitting to your fatigue and can give you a psychological lift as well.

If you become exhausted, of course, or if you start to feel faint or to experience other unusual physical symptoms, stop running and walk until you feel better—or even drop out of the race. It's no disgrace not to finish, and there will be other races. But if the problem is only one of simple fatigue, you may be better off just slowing your pace down to the slowest run possible. Many runners find that once they have started to walk part of the race, they tend to walk more and run less; a very slow run will rest and relax you almost as much as walking, and will make it easier for you to finish running.

Finally, remember that no matter how long the race, and no matter how near the back of the pack you are, you are one of a minority of people who can run a race of any sort and finish it. And believe me, that experience can do almost as much for your general running and all-round self-esteem as finishing first in a field of eight hundred.

What It's Like to Run a Race

I ran my first race in the third Mini-Marathon in 1974, at the age of thirty. Although I'd been hearing about the Mini for months, I didn't actually decide to enter it until ten days before it was run; the farthest distance I had actually run before this was a little over three miles, and I had not done this distance regularly. Still, I was running around ten miles a week, and it seemed at least possible, if not very likely, that I might actually finish the race.

To ensure that I would be able to get through this "grueling" event, I enlisted my friend Ted, a former college competitive runner, to give me pointers on running; and my friend Fern, whom I badgered until she finally agreed to enter the Mini with me.

To train, since we had so little time, Ted took us out to the park and ran us around the course once—"to prove to you," as he said later, "that you could do it." During this training run we did not run the whole course continuously, of course, but we did run and walk all of it, including the fierce hills that have discouraged many people from running in Central Park. Much to my surprise, I found that it was a great deal easier to *run* uphill than to bike up those same hills. A little reflection told me the reason is that when you're biking a hill, you're pulling the weight of your bike as well as your own weight up an incline against the pull of gravity. Ted stressed again and again as Fern and I huffed and puffed that we must *relax* and remember we were going into the race to have a good time. After taking us around the park that day, he assured us both that we would definitely be able to finish the Mini.

The day of the race was a perfect warm, sunny May day. Fern and I had both agonized about what to wear, and we both ended up wearing exactly what we always wear to train in: shorts and leotards. In addition, I wore a tennis hat to protect myself against sunburn. When

Fern and I met at the Y for check-in, we looked at each other and laughed: both of us were wearing make-up, and she had added perfume. "After all," she said, "I may be a jock, but I still want to look feminine."

The pre-race period was taken up with registering and getting our numbers, pinning them on and then going to the bathroom. (For some reason, beginning runners tend to feel a need to go to the bathroom about ten times before a race.) Then we both went out into the park where dozens of women were gathered and began to get caught up in the excitement. We were really going to do it! We were going to run a six-mile race!

Some of the women were jogging slowly to warm up, others were doing stretching exercises (which Fern and I did too, for a while, until we got bored), still others were standing around just chatting in nervousness and excitement, or posing for snapshots.

Finally, the moment arrived. One hundred fifty-seven women crowded behind the starting line, waiting for the gun—and we were off!

Fern and I had decided the day before that we would try not to run fast but would run at our normal pace, to make sure we would finish. So we started out slowly down the long, low hill which begins the course, watching in amazement as dozens of women took off at jackrabbit speed and were soon lost to sight around the first bend. With false confidence I tried to relax and get into a groove of running, but it wasn't working. Finally I turned to Fern and asked diffidently, "Well, how do you feel?" "Lousy," she answered. "How about you?"

With this we both laughed and relaxed, and after another few minutes both of us did loosen up and settle into a comfortable pace. Once we were in our groove, we began to chat together and with other women we passed or who passed us. Then, about three miles into the race, there suddenly appeared ahead of us a water station. Even though I had known that water would be provided along the route, I somehow had never considered what that would actually mean. Volunteers were handing out paper cups of water to the women who ran by. Some women stopped and sipped, while others drank as they continued to run. When Fern and I received our paper cups, she managed to sip hers and get most of it down while running, but I found it absolutely impossible to drink a drop: the bouncing motion of my body kept sending the water into my eye or down my front instead of into my parched mouth. Not wanting to stop, I finally gave up and poured the rest of the water over my head—and it felt great! Somehow it was just the cooling lift I needed to relax and get back into the race.

Fern and I were both surprised to find that very few bystanders made insulting or embarrassing comments as we ran; most remarks, in fact, were encouraging: such as, "Only four miles to go!" "God bless you, girls," and the like.

About four miles into the race, I suddenly developed a side stitch. I told Fern I had to slow down, and she slowed with me. After a very short while the stitch passed and we picked up our speed. Then, up ahead, loomed "Heartbreak Hill," the steep, seemingly endless hill that stands about two-thirds of the way through the course. Fern and I were both tired by this time, and I was sure that I would never be able to do it. Sure enough, about halfway up the hill, I started to feel dizzy. With visions of heat prostration running through my head, I told Fern to go on, that I was going to walk. She encouraged me to continue, but I felt I simply couldn't do it, and so I slowed to a walk for the rest of the way up the hill, while Fern ran on.

Just before I reached the crest of the hill, two women who had run with us earlier, from the "U. Mass. Amphibians" according to their T-shirts, approached me and slowed, then asked if I was all right. Weakly, I nodded. "Then come on, sister," they urged. "Run! We know you can make it: we're with you."

At the top of the hill I started running again, while the two U. Mass. Amphibians ran on, eventually passing into the distance. Soon I could again see Fern up ahead of me, but by this time I was very tired, and since I didn't want to have to walk again, I just followed her, drawing a vague comfort from the fact that she was at least within sight. At the next water station I again poured water on my head, which again refreshed me, and just when I was feeling so tired that I didn't think I could possibly finish, a man up ahead called out, "Only one more mile. You're nearly finished."

Only one more mile? At this point, even one more block would have seemed too much. How could I possibly go on? Trying not to think about the impossible distance of one mile, I concentrated on putting one foot ahead of the other, sure that at any moment I would drop out. Soon there were very few yards between me and Fern, and I couldn't see anyone else on the road, either ahead of us or behind. Were we the last two runners in the race, I wondered? In the world? What was I doing this for, anyway? Was I out of my mind? What was I trying to prove? Run six miles? Who needed it? Once again, I was on the verge of giving up, when finally, in the distance, there it was: the finish line! The route along the way was lined with what looked like hundreds of spectators. Surely they weren't still watching the Mini? It must have been over hours ago. But there was no mistaking the cheering when I suddenly found myself running between those two walls of people, with their encouraging shouts of "Come on, just a few more yards! Keep going! You can do it!" And then I was across the finish line, right behind Fern, while men and women, many of whom had earlier finished the race, clapped and cheered and hugged us.

We hadn't even done that badly: we'd finished 121 and 122, out of a field of one hundred fifty-seven women. Pretty good for two formerly unfit health runners who had only wanted to finish.

Because of the tremendous psychological lift you get just from running it, the Mini-Marathon is an especially good race for women who aren't interested in frequent competition. Most of the women I know who have run the Mini feel it was one of the most worthwhile things they have ever done in their lives, whether they finished in the top fifty or the last ten.

Though most of the entrants are health runners like Fern and me, or women who enjoy racing just for the fun of it, like the women from the U. Mass. Amphibians, many top women runners from all over the world also enter the Mini, to tune up for other races or to try to win or set records.

Nina Kuscsik, one of the original organizers of the first Mini, still runs it every year and still loves it, but her main event is the full marathon. In fact, Kuscsik has run over thirty-five marathons in her life and was the first winner of the women's division at Boston in 1972, the year the Marathon was first officially opened to women.

Kuscsik began running competitively in her thirties partly because she had always been active athletically and partly because she had played many competitive sports in the past. But the demands of work, housekeeping and three children gradually pushed her into running as the only sport she had time for.

After Kuscsik finished at Boston in 1972, she says all she could think about as she sat huddled in a blanket and faced endless interviews about what it felt like to be the first woman winner was how sick she was: thirteen miles into the race, she had begun to develop stomach cramps and then diarrhea. "I thought about stopping," she reports, "but never seriously. I wanted to win—even more than that, I felt I *deserved* to win. At one point while I was being interviewed I told the reporters that I had never before realized how truly competitive I was; they took that to mean that it was unusual for a woman to want to beat other women in a long-distance race. What I was talking about, of course, was the fact that I had run thirteen miles through the streets of Boston while desperately ill: I had proved to myself that I really had guts, and I had found out something about myself that I had never known before."

Kuscsik believes it's true for any woman that "you never really know yourself until you have run a race as hard as you can." For whether you run the Boston Marathon or just take part in an occasional two-mile fun run, you will learn the limits of your own mental and physical capabilities only by testing them—against yourself and against others.

Afterword

"**C**AUTION: running can be addicting." Although that label is not likely to appear on the soles of running shoes, anyone who has run consistently for more than a few months knows it is true. The longer you run, the more you find that you want and need that workout for the relaxation of your body and the tranquillity of your mind.

When I first began running, all I cared about was improving my deteriorating health. And now, nearly five years later, I still marvel when I think about how completely I have changed. In many ways I am a different person: healthy, full of energy, firm and fit. From time to time I meet someone I haven't seen for a few years, and the response is always the same: "You look great—so healthy!" or "How do you do it? You haven't aged a bit." But this isn't unusual—every runner I know is a living advertisement for the benefits of running.

Far more important than the improvement in my health and appearance is the change in my outlook on life. I no longer fear aging as an inevitable process of decline, because I know that as long as I continue to run, my body and mind will respond by staying as young and vigorous as possible. In short, I have become an athlete, in the best sense of the word.

As I've become more deeply involved in the world of running, I've come to believe that runners approach the ancient Greek ideal for athletes: development of mind, body and spirit for their own sake, because each human is an integrated, perfectible being. Even in serious competition this ideal is maintained. Runners share a camaraderie almost unique in sports: though each tries to do her or his best, there is also a sincere joy from the attainments of fellow runners. The mutual support and enthusiasm of all participants in the Mini-Marathon is an embodiment of this spirit. Though running can be a solitary sport for those who enjoy solitude, the long-distance runner need never be lonely. For whether you run alone or with friends, you share a bond with all other runners everywhere, from health runners to marathon champions.

As you continue to run you will find, as I do, that there are always new goals to set for yourself—from the simplest one of continuing to run to the heady thought of maybe someday trying a marathon, just for the experience. Though Boston is still a distant fantasy for me and most women, I know now that if I really wanted to do it, I could, because my mind and body, which used to seem completely beyond my control, have far fewer limits than I ever dreamed.

Appendix

I. Metric Conversion Tables

Although certain events, such as the mile and the marathon (26+ miles), will probably continue to be run, most international track events have long been measured in the metric system. As the U.S. gradually converts from the English system of measurement, more and more races will be metric, and more metric tracks will be built. The following tables will help you to figure your distance in either system.

A. Miles to Kilometers
(Approximate)

¼ mile	402.3 meters (.4 km)
½ mile	804.7 meters (.8 km)
¾ mile	1,207 meters (1.2 km)
1 mile	1,609 meters (1.6 km)
2 miles	3.2 km

3 miles	4.8 km
4 miles	6.4 km
5 miles	8 km
6 miles	9.6 km
7 miles	11.3 km
8 miles	12.9 km
9 miles	14.5 km
10 miles	16 km

B. Kilometers to Miles
(Approximate)

1 km	.6 mile
1.5 km	.94 mile (metric mile)
2 km	1.25 miles
3 km	1.9 miles
4 km	2.5 miles
5 km	3.1 miles
6 km	3.8 miles
7 km	4.4 miles
8 km	5 miles
9 km	5.6 miles
10 km	6.2 miles
11 km	6.8 miles
12 km	7.4 miles
13 km	8.1 miles
14 km	8.7 miles
15 km	9.3 miles
16 km	10 miles

II. Heart Rate Table

In Chapter 4 I mentioned an easy rule of thumb for figuring your approximate training heart rate. Most experts feel that it is safest and most beneficial if you exercise with your pulse within a range called the "target zone." To find your target zone, use the following guidelines.

1. Subtract your age from 220. This will give you your maximum heart rate, the highest rate your heart can beat before collapse. For example, if you are 32, then your maximum heart rate is 188.

2. Your target zone, the pulse range within which you should train for aerobic benefits, is between 70% and 85% of the figure arrived at in step one. For a thirty-two-year-old, this would be a range of 133–160 heart beats per minute. The upper figure, 160, is called the cut-off heart rate, and you should not exercise above that rate; if after exercise you find that your heart rate is above or near the cut-off rate, slow down until you are in better condition.

Note: Some doctors feel that it is not necessary to exercise in the upper ranges of the target zone, or indeed over a heart rate of 130 beats per minute. Further, the heart rate varies for different people, depending on a variety of factors; consider the figures in the table only approximate guidelines.

Heart Rate Table

Age	Maximum Rate	Cut-Off Rate	Target Zone
	(all numbers in heart beats per minute)		
20	200	170	140–170
25	195	166	137–166
30	190	162	133–162
35	185	157	130–157
40	180	153	126–153
45	175	149	123–149
50	170	145	119–145
55	165	140	116–140
60	160	136	112–136
65	155	132	109–132
70	150	128	105–128

III. Shoe Company Directory

Every month, shoe manufacturers old and new come out with improved lines of running shoes. For the latest information on the best shoes, see *Runner's World*; the October issue each year includes a special supplement which compares all shoes submitted for evaluation. The following list, from *Runner's World*, gives the names and addresses of major distributors of running shoes. Many of these companies sell shoes by mail; but be sure to write first for a catalogue and to see if a foot tracing is requested for a proper fit.

Adidas. Libco, 1 Silver Court, Springfield, NJ 07081; Clossco Inc.,
    2200 Martin Ave., P.O. Box 229, Santa Clara, CA 95050; Vanco, 5133
    West Grand River Ave., P.O. Box 870, Lansing, MI 48901; Hughesco,
    Inc., 2830 Merrell Rd., Dallas TX 75229; Adidas Canada Ltd., 550
    Oakdale Rd., Downsview, Ontario M3N 1W6, Canada
Brooks. Brooks Shoe Manufacturing Co., Factory St., Hanover, PA 17331
Eaton. Charles A. Eaton Co., 147 Centre St., Brockton, MA 02403
E.B. Sport International (Lydiard). Sport International, 6117 Reseda Blvd.,
    Reseda, CA 91335
Econo-Jet. Econo-Jet Sport Shoe Co., 1501 College Ave., S.E., Grand
    Rapids, MI 49502
Karhu. Carlsen Import Shoe Corp., 524 Broadway, New York, NY 10012
Kingswell. Kingswell, Steuben Rd., Peekskill, NY 10566
New Balance. New Balance Athletic Shoes, Inc., 38-42 Everett St.,
    Boston, MA 02135
Nike. Blue Ribbon Sports, 6175 112th, Beaverton, OR 97005; Blue Ribbon
    Sports, 4 Jeffrey Ave., Holliston, MA 01746
Osaga. Osaga, 2620 W. 10th Pl., Eugene, OR 97402
Patrick. Action and Leisure Inc., 45 E. 30th St., New York, NY 10016
Puma. Beconta Inc., 50 Executive Blvd., Elmsford, NY 10523; Beconta
    Inc., 340 Oyster Point Blvd., South San Francisco, CA 94080;
    Beconta Inc., 6759 East 50th Ave., Commerce City, CA 90022
Reebok. Bradford Distributors, P.O. Box 356, Huntington Valley, PA 19006
Saucony. Saucony, 12 Peach St., Kutztown, PA 19530
Spotbilt. Spotbilt, 4320 Columbia, Cambridge, MA 02140
Tiger. Onitsuka, 13512 Newhope St., Garden Grove, CA 92643

IV. Organizations for Runners

National Jogging Association
1910 K Street, NW
Suite 202
Washington, DC 20006
202-785-8050

This organization is primarily for health runners, though competitive
runners are welcome to join. The fifteen-dollar yearly dues cover member-
ship, including a subscription to the newsletter (published eight times a
year) and a ten-percent discount on books on fitness and sports offered
through the Association.

Road Runners Club of America, an organization dedicated to distance running and jogging for sport and physical fitness, has seventy-five clubs all over the country. RRCA publishes a quarterly newsletter and promotes many races at varying distances open to runners of all levels and ages. For further information, send a self-addressed, stamped envelope to

Stuart J. Brahs, 803 Brice Road, Rockville, MD 20852, or

Jeff Darman, 2737 Devonshire Pl., NW, Washington, DC 20008

V. Books and Magazines

Aerobics for Women, by Mildred and Kenneth H. Cooper. Bantam, 1972, $1.50.

This book, based on the earlier *Aerobics* and *New Aerobics*, fully explains the theory of the aerobic conditioning and provides a large number of charts that give graduated programs in all aerobic exercises and allow easy comparison between the different types of aerobic exercises. The original *Aerobics*, based on research Dr. Cooper did with hundreds of Air Force men, helped start the "jogging revolution" of the sixties.

Women's Running, by Joan Ullyot. World Publications, 1976, $3.95 ($5.95 hardcover).

In this book, Dr. Ullyot, an M.D. and frequent marathoner, discusses the special problems of women's running, with emphasis on long-distance racing. Especially valuable for women competitors is her discussion of popular men's training schedules adapted for women. *Women's Running* is available by mail order from World Publications, P.O. Box 366, Mountain View, CA 94040.

YMCA Fitness Handbook, by Clayton R. Myers. Popular Library, 1975, $1.50.

This book gives a wide variety of exercises for muscular and skeletal conditioning and advocates a comprehensive approach to fitness.

Runner's World

The best source for continuing information on running, from competitive long-distance racing to running for health, is *Runner's World* magazine, published monthly. In addition to the results of all important long-distance races in the country, *Runner's World* features articles on all aspects of the sport from the psychological to the medical. Available by subscription only from World Publications, P.O. Box 366, Mountain View, CA 94040. A year's subscription costs $9.50; back issues are $1.00 each.

Runner's World also publishes an excellent series of booklets on all aspects of running; for further information, write the publisher at the above address.

Index